# FROM PRINT TO EBOOKS

# A HYBRID PUBLISHING TOOLKIT FOR THE ARTS

DIGITAL PUBLISHING TOOLKIT

## COLOPHON

**AUTHORS** DPT Collective, consisting of: Marc de Bruijn, Liz Castro, Florian Cramer, Joost Kircz, Silvio Lorusso, Michael Murtaugh, Pia Pol, Miriam Rasch and Margreet Riphagen **EDITORS** Florian Cramer, Joe Monk, Miriam Rasch and Amy Wu **IMAGES** Medamo and Kimmy Spreeuwenberg **PRINT DESIGN** Medamo and Kimmy Spreeuwenberg **EPUB DESIGN** André Castro **COVER DESIGN** Medamo and Kimmy Spreeuwenberg **PRINTER** Drukkerij Printvisie B.V., Rotterdam **PUBLISHER** Institute of Network Cultures, Amsterdam **SUPPORTED BY** SIA National Regieorgaan Praktijkgericht Onderzoek **AN EPUB AND PDF EDITION OF THIS PUBLICATION ARE FREELY DOWNLOADABLE FROM** http://networkcultures.org/publications/ **ORDER A COPY OF THIS BOOK BY EMAIL** books@networkcultures.org **CONTACT** Institute of Network Cultures, Hogeschool van Amsterdam, Rhijnspoorplein 1, 1091 GC Amsterdam, The Netherlands http://www.networkcultures.org books@networkcultures.org, t: +31 (0)20 595 18 65


For background material, blog posts, videos and the software created within this Digital Publishing Toolkit project please visit: http://networkcultures.org/digitalpublishing.

Throughout the book the following symbol will appear, pointing to blog posts relevant to the discussed topic: ◺
Underscored words are explained in the Glossary.

Amsterdam, 2015
ISBN 978-90-822345-3-4 (print)
ISBN 978-90-822345-4-1 (EPUB)

# FROM PRINT TO EBOOKS

# A HYBRID PUBLISHING TOOLKIT FOR THE ARTS

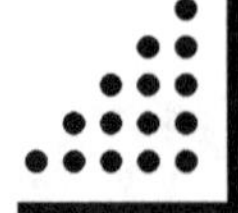

# 00

# CONTENTS

# 01

# INTRO-DUCTION

- Hybrid print and electronic publishing requires new work methods and workflows.

- Low-budget, small-edition, visually-oriented publications that are designed in-house will require more significant changes in work methods than big-budget publications for which the ebook design can be outsourced.

- Interactive multimedia is still difficult to realize in books. Yet there are new opportunities for entirely new publication formats (such as books with customized content and micro-books).

- This Toolkit focuses on low-budget, hybrid print and electronic books designed in-house using standard software and Open Source tools.

'You must change your life' – borrowing from the philosopher Peter Sloterdijk, this could be the summary of our message to art-oriented and design-oriented publishers, writers, editors and designers who are currently transitioning from traditional book making to electronic publishing or – more typically – hybrid publishing of print and electronic formats. Hybrid publishing will sooner or later confront them with the need to re-think traditional publication formats, editorial and production workflows, and distribution. The changes required may well be greater and more extensive than initially expected!

*Change will be minor for scientific publishers and large publishers*

Having said that, there are exceptions. Workflow changes can be also minor for publishers who already do all their editorial work in highly structured digital document formats such as XML or databases; but this is typically only the case in scientific and technology-oriented publishing. Changes may also be minor for larger publishers who can afford outsourcing. Generating an electronic (digital) publication in parallel to a printed publication is then simply a matter of paying an external service provider, such as a document engineering company or a media design agency, to turn a Microsoft Word or Adobe InDesign file into an ebook. This process can be quick if the book is visually simple – such as a novel or a textbook with few illustrations – and economically worthwhile if many ebooks will be sold.

*Change will be major for small, arts-oriented publishers*

Since this Toolkit – consisting of this manual and an online software kit[1] – is meant for publishers who publish visually oriented books in mostly smaller print runs, we propose here an alternative to the process mentioned above. Neither a complex internal IT infrastructure, nor costly outsourcing will be viable solutions for these types of publishers. Unfortunately, there is no 'magic' software button that will turn a print book design into an electronic publication just like that. Since the two media are so different, each with its own specific editorial and visual design needs, such a button is unlikely to materialize in the future either. Hybrid publishing will ultimately require changes in the way the editorial work is done. The good news is that such change is possible. This Toolkit includes instructions on how to deal with the many issues that arise when making the transition from traditional to hybrid or electronic publishing.

1 Digital Publishing Toolkit, http://networkcultures.org/digitalpublishing/toolkit.

For art and design publishers, the challenge of 'going electronic' with their publications is greater than that faced by other fields of publishing, for a number of reasons:

- Visually oriented publications are still more difficult to realize technically in the electronic medium, particularly when designing for a multitude of different reading devices and ebook platforms.
- Small publishers are under a great deal of pressure to keep project costs low, often due to smaller budgets. However, the need to publish in multiple forms (print and electronic) will inevitably increase costs, unless one does as much work as possible in a way that is not dependent on the medium.
- In order to make the investment in an electronic publication durable, electronic publications must be sustainable: they should not require constant investment in technical maintenance and version updates.

## INDUSTRY PROMISES VS. REALITY

There is a stark contrast between the fanciful promises of the computer industry and the often harsh reality of the new digital medium. On one hand, publishers, editors, designers and artists tend to overestimate the interactivity and multimedia possibilities of electronic publishing. These extra possibilities do exist, but in most cases bring with them higher development costs and remain specific to one particular technical platform.

On the other hand, publishers tend to underestimate how even technically simple and seemingly trivial types of electronic publications can in fact lead to a re-thinking of established publishing practices and formats. When traditional publishing formats are replaced by electronic or hybrid formats, there is a real possibility for transformation. Once the book becomes electronic or hybrid, the permanence, immutability and stability typical of physical books is likely to mutate into dynamic, modular, and participative forms. Such publications can greatly benefit from the networked environment in which ebooks exist.

Various types of electronic publications may be subject to different kinds of change. Still, the change will always radical. An exhibition catalog for instance can be split up into interrelated micro-monographs which readers can download and read as individual ebooks. An ebook can be assembled from a variety of sources selected by individual readers, as is currently the case with Wikipedia, where visitors to the website can compile their own collection of Wikipedia articles and export this compilation to an EPUB or PDF document using the Book Creator tool.

The possibilities for change can go beyond the rethinking of existing publishing formats, eventually even redefining what a book actually is.

## WHAT THIS TOOLKIT PROVIDES

'Going electronic' – or going hybrid – requires changing the way you work during the publishing process, from delivered manuscript to final publication. The software tools currently in use, from word processors such as Microsoft Word to desktop publishing (DTP) suites such as Adobe InDesign, were created for the world of analog print and desktop publishing. Although it is entirely possible to create electronic publications from Microsoft Word documents ◺ *(Converting a Docx directly to EPUB using Calibre)* or InDesign documents, ◺ *(Notes on EPUB Development in Adobe InDesign CS6)* which are likely to be the standard format used in existing publishing workflows, in most cases this will be a painful, slow, inefficient and expensive process. This Toolkit focuses instead on do-it-yourself (DIY) technical alternatives. Firstly because the Toolkit is primarily aimed at publishers who, in most cases, cannot afford to outsource ebook design to external service providers; secondly because it is aimed at those who wish to keep the design process in their own hands.

This Toolkit focuses particularly (but not exclusively) on EPUB3 as an electronic publication format, and on Markdown as a word processing format, because of the specific needs of small-edition publishers in the field of art and design: low costs, ease of use, sustainability, and platform independence. The recommendations stem from our practical experience in collaborating on electronic publication projects with four Dutch art, design and research publishers: BIS Publishers, Valiz, nai010 Publishers and the Institute of Network Cultures.

## WHO IS THIS TOOLKIT WRITTEN FOR

You may be a publisher, a designer, or someone who is just starting out with making books. You probably identify with, or work in, the arts. You may be hoping to find answers, gain knowledge, pick up some tips, and consult various resources. This Toolkit intends to provide all of that. The overall focus is on pragmatic solutions for publishers within the sector of art and culture. No prior knowledge of creating an ebook is required. Having said that, a familiarity with various computer software applications is certainly helpful, as is the willingness to learn, and an inquisitive curiosity to look beyond this guide for specific answers. This publication is not meant as a complete tutorial on how to create an electronic publication; rather, it intends to provide the reader with basic guidance on how to make a first attempt at creating such a publication.

As we said at the beginning of this introduction, 'you must change your life'; therefore, you may experience something of a culture shock as you read through this document. If electronic publishing is to be merely an afterthought in the production chain and the product portfolio, the amount of change may be relatively small. However, if electronic publishing is to become just as important as print, the change may be quite radical. In other words, if you are seriously interested in electronic publishing, you must be willing to change your current way of working, and to gradually familiarize yourself with the less mainstream alternatives offered here.

## HOW TO USE THIS TOOLKIT

The Toolkit aims to provide a practical guide on how to develop electronic publications, for publishers as well as for anyone else interested in this subject matter. The Toolkit will attempt to provide insight into the prerequisite conditions of electronic publishing, to suggest Open Source tools whenever possible, and to allow publishers active in the art and culture sector to navigate the diverse and complex landscape of digital publishing in a more informed way.

Furthermore, the Toolkit will help the reader to develop electronic publications – specifically art and design publications, which generally make use of a greater variety of fonts, graphics and layout than publications focused exclusively or mainly on text.

After a basic exploration in Chapter 2 of publishing in general and electronic publishing in particular, in Chapter 3 we provide a general introduction to electronic publishing, sketching out various scenarios on how to develop electronic publications and discussing a number of issues and opportunities in 'going electronic'. In Chapter 4 we focus on the strengths and limitations of various specific types of e-reader hardware and software as well as different file formats, before moving on to describe in Chapter 5 a number of distribution platforms. In Chapter 6 we provide a step-by-step guide to creating your own EPUB. Chapter 7 offers a practical, how-to guide for workflows (both generally structured and specific to each scenario) and finally in Chapter 8 we explore the design of electronic publications for the various scenarios addressed earlier. Finally, in Chapter 9 we look into the future of electronic publishing. The manual also includes a description of the software developed within the different project groups, and a glossary of terms.

We wish to stress here that the structure of the manual is not as linear as the above outline may suggest. Particularly further on in the manual, some of the terminology may seem confusing at first, but will be explained in more detail later.

## WHO WORKED ON THIS TOOLKIT

This publication is an outcome of the two-year research and development project Digital Publishing Toolkit funded by the Dutch Stichting Innovatie Alliantie (SIA) as part of its[2] RAAK-MKB[3] program for innovation in small and medium-sized businesses. The project was based on the following research question: *In what way can a platform be created with new tools for Open Source publishing that will allow publishers in the sector of art and culture to produce interactive e-publications themselves?*

To answer this research question, the Institute of Network Cultures (lectoraat Netwerkcultuur) of the Amsterdam University of Applied Sciences, together with the Research Centre Creating 010 (kenniscentrum Creating 010) of the

2 Blog of the Digital Publishing Toolkit research program, http://networkcultures.org/digitalpublishing.

3 Nationaal Regieorgaan Praktijkgericht Onderzoek SIA, http://www.regieorgaan-sia.nl.

Rotterdam University of Applied Sciences jointly conducted state-of-the-practice-oriented design research. In collaboration with an already existing consortium[4] of eleven small businesses including publishers, designers and developers, four sub-projects were formulated. Within these sub-projects, a number of collaborations took place between publishers, designers, developers, researchers, and students of the participating universities of applied sciences.

The result is the present publication, as well as a software repository consisting of tools for electronic publishing, based on Open Source software of which the source code is published and freely accessible.[5] With a single command line, one can get hold of the code repository, downloading not only the current state of 'source' files for the book, but also the full history of changes and comments made by each collaborator to the Toolkit up to that point. With another command, the various 'sources' can be pulled together into an instantly produced EPUB document. In this way both the 'content' and the 'machine' used for making the book are bundled and shared.

We are not claiming that all ebooks will follow, or indeed should follow this path. We are simply laying out one of the many directions ebook creators can now take with their publications, by using simple and inexpensive tools, and without having to buy into the industry's glossy promises of multimedia and interactivity.

4 Digital Publishing Toolkit consortium, http://networkcultures.org/digitalpublishing/consortium/.

5 Digital Publishing Toolkit GitHub, http://networkcultures.org/digitalpublishing/github/.

# 02

# THE BASICS

- Throughout the historical development of writing, characters beyond the basic alphabet have played an increasingly important role, starting with blank spaces between words, then punctuation marks, and later markup for formatting.

- In electronic texts, markup has developed into two general types: 'What You See Is What You Get' or visual-typographic (as in the markup tag 'bold type') vs. logical-semantic (as in the markup tag 'emphasis').

- Logical-semantic markup is the foundation of hybrid publishing, since it can be translated into whatever visual formatting is most suitable for each particular medium.

- One of the main advantages of electronic books is that the same content can be published in a wide variety of formats.

## LAYOUT AND STRUCTURE OF A TEXT

A text is a collection of words and words are composed of letters. In order to read a text, we make use of a variety of layout aids. The most simple and basic of these is the use of spaces between words. Classical Greek and Roman texts were written in what is called 'continuous script', without spaces, which was not considered a problem since reading was a craft which only a few people mastered. Gradually, an increasing number of design and layout aids were introduced: not only spaces between words but also capital letters at the beginning of sentences, line breaks, and a variety of punctuation marks such as commas, semicolons, colons and periods.[1] Also, concepts such as paragraphs and chapters developed into a standardized system that allowed the structure intended by the authors to be transmitted to readers familiar with these standards.

In the electronic processing of texts, this hierarchical ordering of words into sentences, sentences into paragraphs and so on, as well as additional reading aids such bold or italic text, is made possible by using specific formatting codes. This process is called markup and the codes are called markup elements. It goes without saying that all these markup elements require stable definitions and clear relationships if they are to be of any use. In order to establish which markup is allowed and how it should be used, markup languages were defined.

With the emergence of computer networks and the increasing need to standardize texts for multiple usages, an international ISO standard was defined in 1982, known as Standardized General Markup Language (SGML). This was an extremely important development, as it established a logical-semantic approach, in other words a strict division between the *conceptual* structure and formatting of the text, and the final visual *representation* of that structure and formatting. This is radically different from the 'What You See Is What You Get' (WYSIWYG) markup languages used in word processors such as Microsoft Word, WordPerfect or OpenOffice, where text which is marked up in a certain way (such as italic or bold) is immediately displayed that way, so that there is no visible distinction between the conceptual structure and the visual representation. SGML and its derivatives, HTML (Hypertext Markup Language), used mainly in web design, and the expanded XML (Extensible Markup Language), allow instead for formatting *concepts* such as 'emphasis' or 'strong

1 Guglielmo Cavallo and Roger Chartier (eds.), *A History of Reading in the West,* Polity Press 1999.

emphasis', (rather than 'italic' or 'bold') as well as structuring concepts such as 'chapter heading' or 'quotation', to be linked logically to specific display representations for each concept in a separate list of definitions known as a style sheet (such as Cascading Style Sheets (CSS) in web design).

This is especially important and relevant in the context of hybrid publishing because it makes it possible, at the later stage of visual design, not only to define how each of these markup elements will be displayed, but also to provide different definitions for each specific output. For example, we can decide that for output A (say the printed book), text marked as 'chapter heading' will be centered on the page, in a different font and larger font size than the running text, while text marked as 'quotation' will be rendered in the same font and size as the running text, but in italics; while for output B (say a display screen)

## FROM STRUCTURE TO REPRESENTATION

**STRUCTURE**

The quick brown <strong> fox jumps </strong> over the lazy dog

**STYLES**

**TABLET**
font style: regular
font size: 18 px

**LAPTOP**
font style: bold
font size: 100 px

**SMARTPHONE**
font style: italic
font size: 10 px

**REPRESENTATION**

we could instead decide to render chapter headings as bold and quotations as underlined text.

By combining the structured text with a different style sheet for each output format, a variety of end products can thus be generated using one single structured text. However, in order to make this possible, the source text must be as systematically structured as possible.

## WHAT IS AN ELECTRONIC TEXT?

An electronic text is generally understood as a text which is represented on a display screen of some sort. However, the most important difference between a paper text and an electronic text, in the context of hybrid publishing, is the notion that the electronic text becomes a structured file. As we have seen, the use of markup allows us to create different layouts, or representations, for different media. It is also crucial to understand that electronic publishing introduces a paradigm shift away from the page-centered culture of book printing. Book printing traditionally allows for various printing sizes, depending on the wishes of the author, designer and publisher. For example, when making an art book based on a collection of paintings or drawings, a decision will be made as to what the ideal book size is, and whether it should be printed in portrait or landscape format. In the world of screens however, it is no longer the designer who makes this choice, but the users – depending on whether they choose to read an electronic book on a smartphone, tablet, monochrome e-reader, personal computer, or whatever other device is available. Ideally, the electronic publication can be viewed all of these devices, without the need for any device-specific redesigns.

Most electronic reading devices support reflowable layout (also known as 'responsive' design), which means that the layout of the document is automatically adapted to fit the dimensions of the device. This works well for genres such as novels which usually consist only of text. However when the overall design cannot so easily be modified, for example if there are crucial relationships between the body text and images or other elements such as footnotes or tables (as is the case for art and design books as well as research publications), then the transposition from an existing print work to an electronic representation can pose some serious issues, which will be further addressed in the following chapters.

## POSSIBILITIES OFFERED BY ELECTRONIC PUBLISHING

One of the most widespread forms of electronic publishing consists of scanning existing paper books and converting them into digital media such as images, electronic texts, or an ebook. Optical character recognition (OCR) is often used to convert the printed text of a book into a digital text format such as ASCII or Unicode. After this conversion the text can be re-formatted, searched, or processed using other software applications. Examples of organizations or projects for book scanning on a large scale are: Project Gutenberg,[2] the Million Book Project,[3] Google Books,[4] and the Open Content Alliance.[5]

New electronic technologies allow for a variety of publication outlets, bringing new opportunities as well as new challenges. Page numbering and indexing for example, which for centuries were essential book-making concepts, are problematic in electronic publications, where page numbers are unstable or even non-existent.6 Fixed page numbers and indexes referring to page numbers have traditionally allowed readers, writers and researchers to refer to the same publication (or at least the same edition) across time and space. However, in an electronic environment with non-fixed screen sizes this is much more complicated. Though the text itself usually remains fixed, as the original text file exists independently from its delivery format (e-paper, LCD, paper), the actual visual layout or representation in each format can vary substantially, making it much harder to refer to the location of a passage in the text. The challenge becomes even greater if we widen our ambition to include not only tables, references and notes but also pictures, audio and video, and hyperlinks.

Just as cultural standardization of typography and layout over the centuries has made it possible to instantly distinguish a novel, an educational textbook, or a 'coffee table book' of art reproductions, this will in all likelihood eventually be the case as well for different genres of electronic books. With the notable exception of electronic (or paper) books as art objects in their own

2 Project Gutenberg, https://www.gutenberg.org.

3 Million Book Project, https://archive.org/details/millionbooks.

4 Google Books, http://books.google.nl/.

5 Open Content Alliance, http://www.opencontentalliance.org.

6 A historical illustration of this problem, and a possible solution, is the numbering of chapters and verses in the Bible, allowing readers to refer to the same passage even though they may be using different editions, or even different languages.

right, electronic art book publishing is already quickly developing many common features as a genre, though differences between individual publications will always remain.

At the most basic level, all files in an ebook are nothing but bitstreams (streams of binary code: zeros and ones). As we have seen, the great novelty in the world of electronic art books is that, based on standardized but flexible structures, the same content can be published in a wide variety of formats. This not only depends on the capabilities of the output (reading/viewing/listening) device, but also on the function of the book, such as a dictionary, a study book, a reference work, a catalogue, or a work of fiction.

All these new possibilities will require thorough, and potentially more labor-intensive, editorial and production strategies. Not only because of the possibility of representing the same content in a variety of forms, but more importantly because once they are properly edited and stored electronically, the content and its constituent parts can be endlessly used and re-used in different ways, now and in the future. This also means that electronic publishing will, in most cases, not bring any significant decrease in production costs.

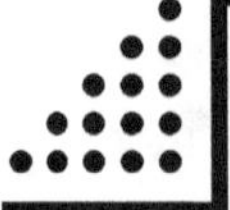

# 03

# GENRES OF PUBLICATION

- In art and design publishing, the most common genres are: research publications, art/design catalogues, artists'/designers' books, and art/design periodicals.

- The opportunities and challenges of electronic publishing are different for each genre.

- Common opportunities include search-ability, ease of access and distribution, and modularization of content; common difficulties include layout consistency, page numbering and referencing, and large file sizes.

- There are 3 ways of creating hybrid books:
  - One-to-one, where the book is one single product published in different media.
  - One-to-many, where the book has different appearances in different media.
  - One-to-database, where the book is based on the content of a database which can be used in a number of ways.

# FIVE GENRES

In the present project we deal with a variety of publication products which we have categorized into five genres:

1. Research publication
2. Art/design catalogue
3. Artists'/designers' book
4. Art/design periodical
5. New genres

## 1. Research publication

- Usually text-based;
- Texts traditionally play a central role;
- Visuals are often secondary (images illustrate the text);
- Often longer texts;
- Often with a standardized structure;
- Often with complex referencing (table of contents, footnotes, endnotes, cross-references, citations, bibliography, keyword and name indexes, list of illustrations, glossary).

**Going electronic: advantages and issues**

In the sciences and humanities, discussions on the digital opportunities for research publications mostly focus on the transition from the traditional textbook to new forms of publication which allow for more complex forms of visualization, inclusion of real-time data, and computation. However, if one wishes to publish in standard ebook formats and target a broad range of electronic reading platforms and devices, the visual and multimedia possibilities offered by current ebook technologies are in fact quite limited – mainly because the ebook files quickly become too large to be downloaded on mobile devices. The alternative, developing research publications as visual apps, will in most cases not be a viable solution since apps have short lifespans of technical compatibility, while research publishing is almost by definition long-term (and long-tail) publishing.

The first, most obvious advantage of 'going electronic' with research publications is that it makes things easier for users: electronic texts make it possible for researchers, students and other readers to search, copy and paste text in a simple and straightforward way. Also, the datasets used in the research can be included within the publication, allowing more serious readers and researchers to engage directly with the research material itself. For publishers, making texts available digitally offers huge advantages in terms of accessibility, particularly on an international level, since distribution of ebooks is not limited by logistical issues of shipment and storage. On the other hand there are also specific problems related to digital research publications. One of these has to do with citation references: without fixed page numbers, there is no standard way of referring to a specific part of the ebook in another publication. This is one reason why scientific ebooks are still often issued as PDFs.

'Going electronic' also opens up new possibilities for creating content. A high degree of standardized structure and ensuing 'modularization' allow for new ways of reading and writing essays. Particularly when different authors refer to each other, they often share data, quotations, tables, figures, etc. Multiple use and reuse of 'modules' can help foster communication within a community. However, this remains a future dream for the time being, since comments and annotations are not linked to (a specific place in) the book the way they are in the case of physical books, which makes sharing more complicated.[1] Another option that comes with modularization is that different users or readers of a text can each extract the modules they need. For example, if we consider an anthology of essays, a user could generate a customized ebook of all bibliographical references within the various texts.

## 2. Art/design catalogue

- Mainly image-based;
- Visuals play a central role;
- Text is secondary (text refers to visuals);
- Descriptive texts of various lengths.

**Going electronic: advantages and issues**

Most art/design catalogues are image-based, and here lies the greatest challenge for electronic publishing in this genre. A publication containing many images with high resolution and high color fidelity will take a long time to

1 Anita de Waard and Joost Kircz, 'Modeling Scientific Research Articles – Shifting Perspectives and Persistent Issues', Proceedings of the 12th International Conference on Electronic Publishing held in Toronto, Canada, 25-27 June 2008, http://elpub.scix.net/data/works/att/234_elpub2008.content.pdf.

download and will occupy a great deal of storage space on the user's device as well as the publisher's servers. And as download speeds and storage space continue to increase exponentially, there is of course an endless temptation to continue increasing the file size accordingly.

Possibilities in this direction lie in offering high-quality 'zoomable' images and adding additional material such as video (documentary, animation, etc.), audio (interviews, lectures, etc.) or even 'interactive' media. Also, most tablet computers offer much better color fidelity than the printed page, a fact which can be used to good advantage when offering ebooks optimized specifically for reading on a tablet. A possible problematic issue is that such catalogues often require a fixed page layout: image and text that belong together should appear next to each other; however, changes in size (of the device or of the user's settings) affect the flow of content, so that the images and text will tend to 'drift apart'.

As with research publications, modularization offers interesting opportunities for writing and presenting material. Since a catalogue often consists of components which are already modular in nature, there is much to be gained from using these features in electronic publishing. For example, by providing readers with the opportunity to 'build' their own publication; by publishing different editions (small, medium, large) of a catalogue with little extra effort; or by easily updating specific parts of the catalogue.

## 3. Artists'/designers' book

- Book *by* an artist, rather than *about* an artist;
- Complex use of images and typography, often pushing the possibilities of the medium;
- In print: making use of the book as a material, visual and tactile object;
- Often difficult or impossible to adapt/convert to other media;
- Text is often used in a non-descriptive or non-narrative way.

**Going electronic: advantages and issues**

Since an artists'/designers' book often constitutes a reflection upon the medium itself, the question of choosing between a digital format or a print edition, of 'going electronic' and weighing the ensuing advantages and issues, does not apply here as it does with other genres. Rather, it is a fundamental choice which will determine from the start many basic characteristics of the book itself. Also, choosing an electronic format such as EPUB for an artists'/designers' book requires a good working knowledge of the specific features of such a format. This seems to be one of the reasons why there are few digital artists' books, if we exclude the electronic (scanned) reproductions of printed artists' books which can be found on repository websites such as UbuWeb[2] and Monoskop.[3]

When working on an electronic edition of an existing printed artists'/designers' book, the choice of the file format is crucial. The end result is to a large extent determined by the specifications of each format, and more generally of each medium. Here too, as with art/design catalogues, one of the main concerns is the quality of the images; another is the relation between text and images.

In the case of artists' books or pamphlets which are not primarily a reflection of their medium (for example Sol LeWitt's 1968 *Sentences on Conceptual Art* which consists of handwritten text on paper pages) and are not particularly difficult to adapt/convert to electronic media, the advantages of doing so are similar to those for other genres: access and distribution, reaching new audiences, the ability to easily copy and paste text and images, and the possibility of incorporating interactive materials.

## 4. Art/design periodical

- Both text-based and image-based;
- Images as well as texts play a central role;
- Use of images is primary as well as secondary;
- Texts of various lengths;
- More or less fixed page layout format;
- Recurring or periodical publication format (e.g. magazines, series etc.).

**Going electronic: advantages and issues**
An important part of the appeal of a periodical is its physical presence. It can be easily picked up from a newsstand or a table, casually tossed in a bag, and eventually disposed of. Though the digital domain has its own ways of inform-

2 UbuWeb, http://www.ubuweb.com.

3 Monoskop, http://monoskop.org/Monoskop.

ing or reminding the readers of a publication's existence and presence (for example, through 'push messages' on tablets and smartphones, e-mail notifications, and sharing via social media) this is of course not quite the same thing.

In terms of archiving, 'going electronic' also provides a number of opportunities and challenges for art/design periodicals. New articles can refer to older ones, and even integrate parts of these older articles. The periodical as such becomes a repository and therefore a breeding ground for new work.

The advantages are mostly the same as with the other genres listed: increased possibilities for extending content (interactivity, video etc.); lower distribution costs; outreach to a larger audience; and modularity. However, storage and download/update speeds can present a challenge, as described earlier.

### 5. New genres

New genres of publication will continue to emerge as a result of the ongoing digitization of the publishing industry. These could fall outside of what we would normally consider a 'book': for example, short pamphlets, poems, essays, sketches, or – in the world of digital media – apps, a series of tweets, a blog, etc. Interactive approaches, similar to adventure games, where the reader is able to control the narrative or to build or customize the publication, have also been imagined and developed since the late 1980s. Up until now, this type of electronic publication (usually known as 'hyperfiction' or 'e-literature') has remained a marginal phenomenon, but one should not exclude the possibility of a resurgence in new contexts.

## THREE LEVELS OF ELECTRONIC PUBLISHING

Independently of the different genres listed above, we can distinguish three levels of electronic publishing. The scope of electronic publishing ranges from the simple conversion of a paper book, to an electronic publication (for example, a PDF of the print edition as an ebook), to full-scale electronic publications which incorporate advanced digital formats such as video, or are published as 'native apps' (applications developed for a particular platform or device). When we consider the different genres of publishing from this perspective, the role and use of metadata also becomes an important factor.

◺ (*Embedding a Custom Set of Metadata Based on Dublin Core Metadata Initiative Into a MultiMarkdown Document*)

Electronic publishing can be divided into three levels, as described in further detail below ◺ (*From Print to What?*):

**1. One-to-one**: the book is considered as a specific product or project where text authors, illustrators, artists, photographers and designers work together to create the book, which then is published as a single edition. The print book can also be converted or adapted into an ebook.

**2. One-to-many**: the publication has a variety of appearances, depending on the context and the available presentation media (type and size of screen/paper). The book is offered in formats such as print, EPUB, PDF, MOBI, web, each with an appearance and functionality suitable to the format being used.

**3. One-to-database**: here the book is not a separate, defined, and limited entity. Rather, a publication is put together from various independent components, defined as modules, which can be used and re-used a number of times by anyone who has access to the database. For example, a user can compile a selection of available chapters and generate a customized ebook.

## 1. One-to-one

On the first level there is the single edition. Each publication is considered as a separate product or project where text authors, illustrators, artists, photographers and designers work together as an ad-hoc team. The production workflow may be unique from book to book, but will usually follow a traditional pattern, from a manuscript to a designed PDF ready to be printed. Images and/or full layout pages are not suitable as reusable (digital) objects. The independent components which together make up the end product are usually not archived separately.

'Going electronic' in this case usually means no more than generating some kind of electronic representation, as accurate as possible, of the printed book. Sometimes the files used for making the printed book will be converted into an EPUB by a third party. This electronic edition is then checked for readability and accuracy of layout (for example, making sure that images and captions are on the same page).

# THREE LEVELS OF ELECTRONIC PUBLISHING

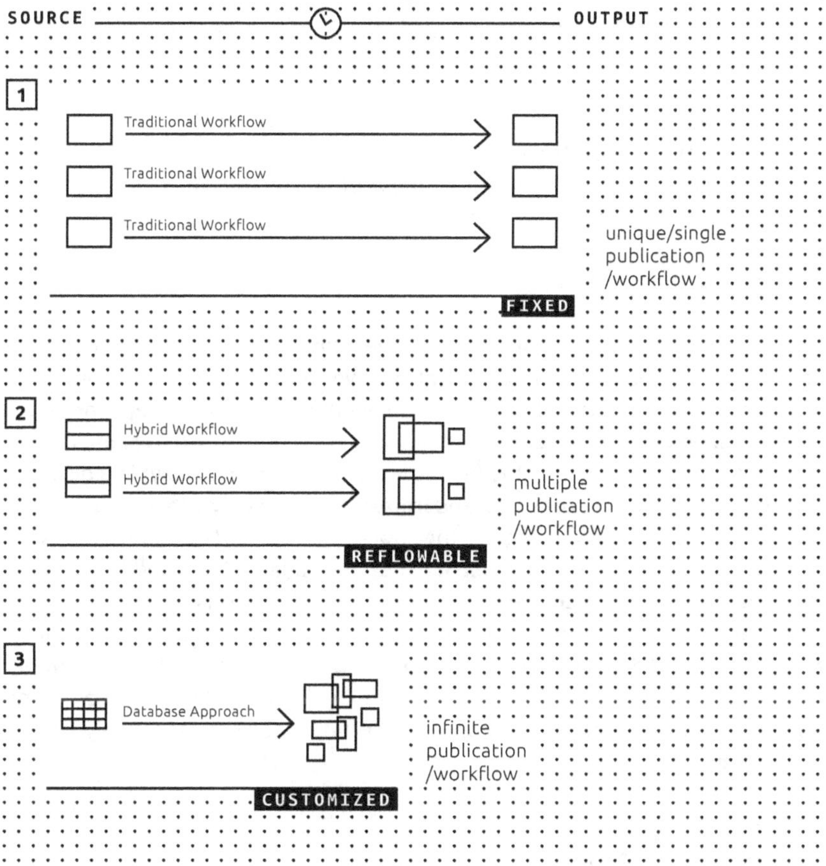

SOURCE — OUTPUT

1

Traditional Workflow

Traditional Workflow

Traditional Workflow

unique/single publication /workflow

FIXED

2

Hybrid Workflow

Hybrid Workflow

multiple publication /workflow

REFLOWABLE

3

Database Approach

infinite publication /workflow

CUSTOMIZED

The publisher may make use of a content management system (CMS), which in its simplest form is just a collection of folders/directories on a hard drive. Archiving is important: often publishers have had to scan their own books for a reprint, simply because they failed to properly archive the files. Maintaining an archive of semantically structured content also offers many new possibilities, not only for efficiently reissuing the publication but also for doing so in new formats which were not previously available.

There are many common characteristics between individual publications within each genre. A better understanding of these characteristics will allow publishers and designers to make good use of new possibilities.

### 2. One-to-many

On the next level we see a split between the manifestation of the (single) printed version, and the (one or many) electronic versions. The electronic version, unlike the paper version, is not a single object but has a different appearance for each ebook format. Also, due to the variety and flexibility of reading devices, different users will see the book differently on their display. The display sizes of reading devices are not standardized and generally allow for both portrait and landscape viewing. Furthermore, the popular (and more or less standard) EPUB allows for reflowable pages and variable fonts and font sizes. Workflow schemes are crucial in one-to-many publications, as the same texts and images will be used across a variety of formats and devices. This requires a structured and detailed workflow, and the use of a set of descriptors (metadata) related to the objects or entities of the publication. Here the ebook is no longer a by-product of the print book, but is produced simultaneously, often in a variety of formats.

### 3. One-to-database

The final level is database publishing, in which all objects or entities of a publication can be used independently of each other. This is possible only when the editorial workflow has defined these objects or entities as individual and unique items within the database, along with the characteristics and features (metadata) of each item.

Particularly for publications which have a more or less fixed layout, database publishing opens up new ways of designing books. For example in the case of a collection of essays, a catalogue, or a journal, readers can compile a personal selection from the available texts. A structured presentation of all material is made possible based on the metadata, allowing readers to navigate and put together a collection based on their own personal interests. Of course this means that tagging, describing, and storing all the components must be done in the early stages of publication and with utmost care.

It is important to note that there will never be one single workflow which fits all requirements. However, by making available the relevant metadata, publications can be created in a variety of formats.

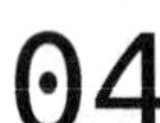

# 04

# TECHNO-LOGIES FOR ELECTRONIC READING

- Users can choose from a multitude of hardware e-reader devices and software e-reader applications.

- The possible combinations of software and hardware are complex and virtually unlimited.

- EPUB is the most common format for electronic books, followed by Amazon's own proprietary ebook formats for its line of Kindle devices.

## READER HARDWARE

There are many ways of viewing electronic publications. Portable devices such as e-readers or tablets are by far the most popular way of accessing such content. Smartphones are, for the purposes of electronic reading, basically miniature versions of their tablet counterparts. Also, large-screen smartphones (called 'phablets') have recently become quite popular, further blurring the distinction between smartphones and tablets. Finally there are desktop computers and laptops which can be used as e-reader devices, sometimes in combination with the physical book: particularly in the case of research publications, a digital version is often used for easy searching and copy/pasting of text selections.

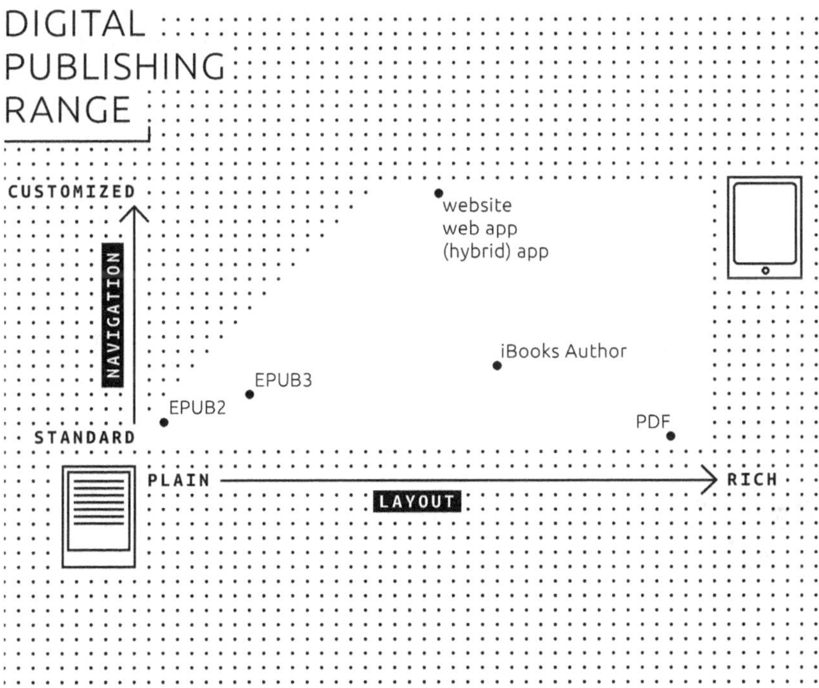

## E-readers

E-readers became widely known with the introduction of Amazon's Kindle in 2007. Standard e-readers, unlike tablets, are only suitable for reading books and are relatively inexpensive. An important characteristic of e-reader devices is the use of a monochrome display technology known as electronic paper (e-paper). Electronic paper is designed to mimic as closely as possible the characteristics of paper, and has a very low energy consumption in comparison with other mobile displays such as the LCD screens used on tablets. The current generation of e-paper is not capable of rendering complex motion, therefore animations and videos cannot be viewed on these devices. Also, the monochrome display means that the current generation of e-readers is mainly suitable for text-based publications, such as novels or research publications.

Some manufacturers of e-readers also offer more expensive models, such as Amazon's Kindle Fire (and Fire HD) or Barnes & Noble's NOOK Tablet (and NOOK HD+). However these models are not really e-readers anymore, but full-fledged, small-sized tablets. Instead of e-paper, they have backlit color LCD screens, a standard feature of tablets such as Apple's iPad and Samsung's Galaxy Tab. Often these models use a version of Android (the most widely

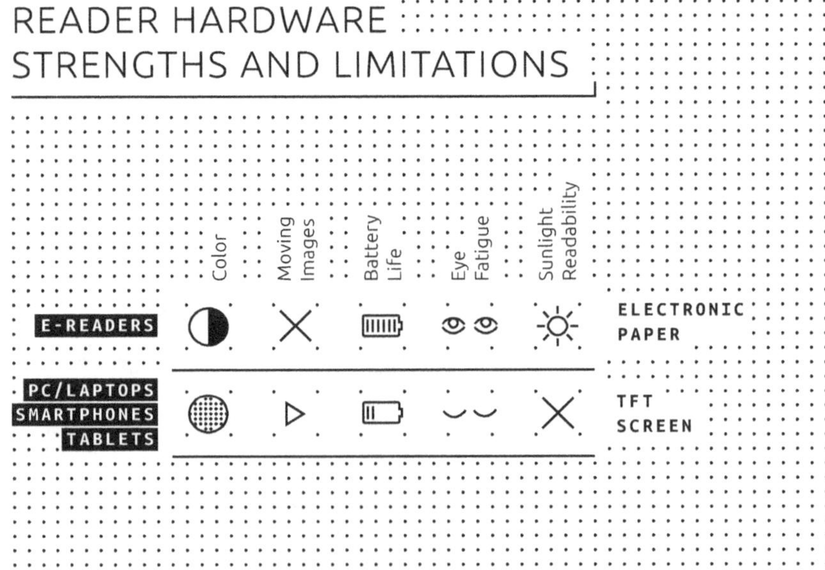

used operating system for mobile devices), in contrast to the traditional monochrome e-readers which use their own operating system, usually derived from a version of Linux. Conversely, Samsung's Galaxy Note and Apple's iPad Mini can be seen as these tablet manufacturers' answer to the smaller-sized e-reading tablets.

## Tablets

The tablet market is currently dominated by two main players, Apple and Samsung.[1] Apple uses its own operating system (iOS) for the iPad, while Samsung has opted for Android as the operating system for its Galaxy Tab product line. In the Android market segment, several manufacturers offer similar hardware with variants of the Android operating system. There are various e-reader software applications for both iOS and Android. We will review the most important of these in the reader software section below.

For viewing arts and design publications, tablets with color LCD screens are far more suitable than e-readers with monochrome e-paper displays. The color fidelity of the newest tablet displays offered by Apple and Samsung is comparable to that of professional monitors used by photographers and graphic designers. However, the tablet's color screen also has some serious drawbacks: backlit LCD screens cause a great deal more eye fatigue than either printed paper or e-paper, while viewing outdoors greatly diminishes image quality. Another issue with tablets is battery life: though newer models continue to provide significant improvements, their relatively large power consumption means they are still no competition in this respect for e-readers, which boast an average battery life of up to several weeks.

## Smartphones

For the purposes of viewing electronic publications, smartphones can be considered broadly similar to tablets, though the screen sizes are of course smaller (and also smaller than those of e-readers). Therefore we have clustered them here together with tablet devices.[2]

1 Gartner Says Worldwide Tablet Sales Grew 68 Percent in 2013, With Android Capturing 62 Percent of the Market, http://www.gartner.com/newsroom/id/2674215.

2 Gartner Says Annual Smartphone Sales Surpassed Sales of Feature Phones for the First Time in 2013, http://www.gartner.com/newsroom/id/2665715.

# ECOLOGIES

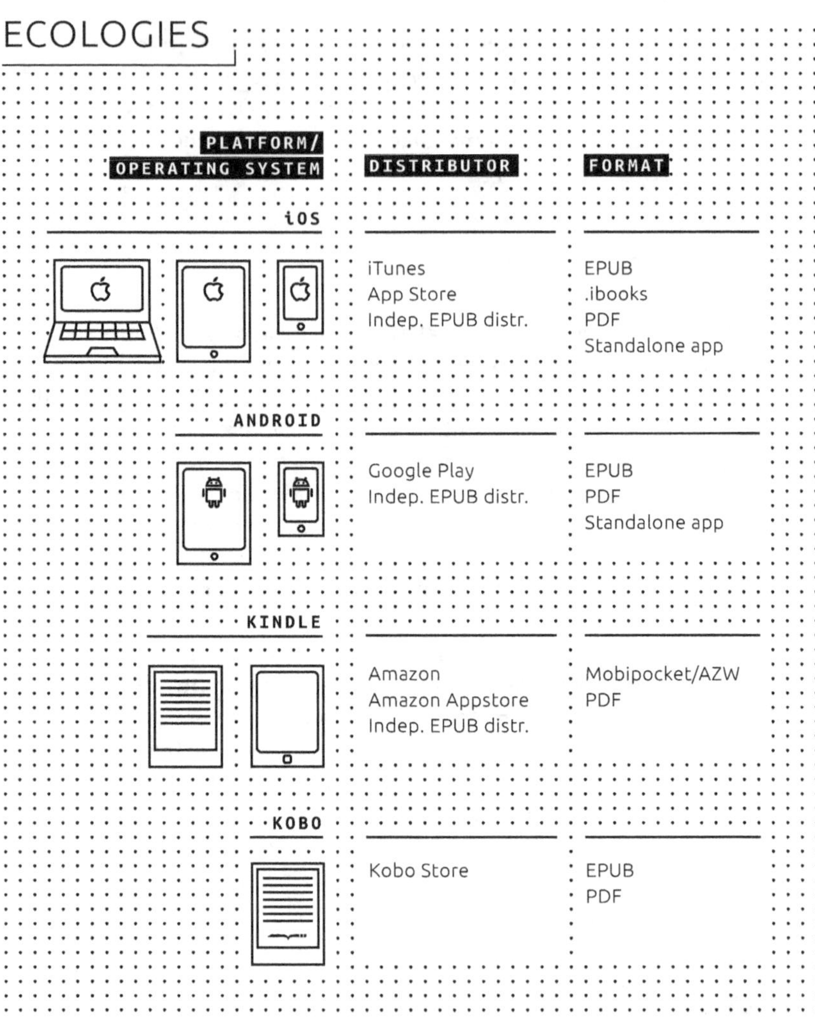

| PLATFORM/ OPERATING SYSTEM | DISTRIBUTOR | FORMAT |
|---|---|---|
| iOS | iTunes<br>App Store<br>Indep. EPUB distr. | EPUB<br>.ibooks<br>PDF<br>Standalone app |
| ANDROID | Google Play<br>Indep. EPUB distr. | EPUB<br>PDF<br>Standalone app |
| KINDLE | Amazon<br>Amazon Appstore<br>Indep. EPUB distr. | Mobipocket/AZW<br>PDF |
| KOBO | Kobo Store | EPUB<br>PDF |

### PCs/laptops

Though ebooks can certainly be read on a laptop or personal computer, this may be ergonomically less natural for the user than reading on a handheld device. The drawbacks of increased eye fatigue and limited battery life are the same as with tablets.

## READER SOFTWARE

Various applications for PCs, tablets and smartphones support an extended subset of the EPUB standard, allowing for extra features such as customized fonts, layout styling, etc. In the following section we will examine the most important applications for electronic reading on mobile devices, desktop and laptop computers, and the web. We distinguish between four 'ecologies', each with its own devices, distribution platforms and software: Apple's iOS, Google's Android, Amazon's Kindle and Kobo.

### Mobile applications

There are various software applications for tablets and smartphones, some of which are 'companion apps' to well-known e-reader devices such as Amazon's Kindle and Kobo's range of e-reader hardware. Other applications were not developed for specific e-reader devices but are integrated into a storefront, such as Apple's iBooks and Aldiko. The applications generally support EPUB2 and EPUB3, though some require the user to convert files into a proprietary file format before the document can be opened, such as the Kindle e-reader device and application which support only Amazon's proprietary file formats (AZW, KF8, MOBI) along with plain text and PDF.

**iBooks**
iBooks is Apple's ebook reader application for iPhone, iPad and Mac OS X. The user can purchase books from the iTunes Store or copy them from another source to the iBooks library. The latest version of iBooks supports many of the features of the EPUB3 standard, as well as PDF and the closed-source .ibooks file format (IBA), which is a derivative of EPUB3.

### Aldiko

Aldiko is both a storefront and ebook reader for Android which supports EPUB and PDF. As such it is comparable to Apple's iBooks. There is a paid version which offers some extra features (annotation, removal of advertisements) not found in the free version.

### Kindle

The Kindle application is Amazon's tablet and smartphone counterpart to their physical e-reader devices. The application is available for both iOS and Android. Books can be bought from inside the application on Android; on iOS the procedure is less straightforward, due to restrictions by Apple on in-app purchasing. Kindle for mobile devices only supports Amazon's proprietary file formats (AZW, KF8) and PDF. EPUBs need to be converted using third-party software (such as Calibre) before Kindle can import the files into its library. The application can sync its library so that a collection of ebooks is available on both the Kindle e-reader and within the application, for example on a smartphone.

### Kobo

Kobo, like Amazon, sells e-reader devices and has a large bookstore. The applications offered for Android and iOS are largely 'companion apps' to Kobo's e-reader devices. Libraries can be synced across devices, provided all the content was purchased in Kobo's bookstore. Kobo supports both EPUB and PDF files.

### Marvin

Marvin is a paid application which focuses mainly on managing existing collections of digital publications compiled from various sources. It does not have its own store. Marvin accepts only EPUB files, but allows users to convert other file formats using third-party software packages such as Calibre.

## PC software

There are also a many desktop applications which make it possible for users to view EPUBs. Of the five applications mentioned above, only Aldiko is not available on desktops, while iBooks is a Mac-only application. Kobo and Kindle both offer Windows and Mac versions of their software – but no Linux version, though Kobo does offer beta software for Debian Linux systems.[3] The functionality is similar to that of the mobile versions.

### Calibre

Calibre is an ebook management suite with a wide variety of features, including a few which are relevant in this particular context. (For a more detailed description of Calibre, see Chapter 6. Calibre provides tools for managing large collections of ebooks, converting files to and from various formats (both ebook[4] and other formats),[5] viewing all major ebook file formats, and even editing EPUB and AZW documents.

### Adobe Digital Editions

Adobe Digital Editions (ADE) is an ebook reader and management tool which can read EPUB and PDF documents. However, support for EPUB3 is incomplete; although Adobe claims that all the important features are supported, it doesn't elaborate on what these important features are. ADE also integrates with many e-reader devices and reader applications which provide syncing possibilities. Therefore a library managed with ADE could, at least in theory, be synced with a compatible device or application.[6]

## Web platforms

There are several web platforms for reading EPUBs online, but their popularity is difficult to estimate. A project called Bookworm, developed by Threepress in 2008, was taken over by O'Reilly Labs in early 2009 and eventually shut down in 2012.[7] The website now describes Bookworm as an 'interesting and useful experiment' and attributes the closure to dramatic changes in the ebook ecosystem over the past few years. Booki.sh, another project, is still online and offers a complete library of ebooks which can be viewed and

---

3 MobileRead, Any interest in Kobo Desktop for Linux?, 5 March 2010, http://www.mobileread.com/forums/showthread.php?t=82378.

4 Converting a Docx directly to EPUB using Calibre, http://networkcultures.org/digitalpublishing/2014/03/28/converting-a-docx-directly-to-epub-using-calibre/.

5 Ebooks manual Calibre, http://manual.calibre-ebook.com/faq.html#what-formats-does-calibre-support-conversion-to-from.

6 Digital Editions Supported Devices, http://blogs.adobe.com/digitalpublishing/supported-devices.

7 Bookworm, "an experimental platform for storing and reading ePub-format books online," is closed as of March 31, 2012, http://oreilly.com/bookworm.

stored online.[8] However it does not appear to be operating commercially, and the ability to purchase books was removed in June 2013.[9]

### Browser applications

Besides web applications, there are also several browser extensions which allow users to read EPUBs in their web browser. However these extensions can best be understood as a convenient way of quickly viewing or previewing ebooks, rather than full-fledged e-reader applications.

**Readium**
Readium is a project by various publishers and technology companies aiming to provide a reference system, a collection of best practices, for rendering EPUB3 publications.[10] Readium offers a range of tools for online and offline use, mainly geared towards software developers. One of these tools is a browser extension[11] for the Google Chrome web browser, allowing users to view an EPUB document inside the browser window.

**EPUBReader**
EPUBReader is similar to the browser extension offered by Readium. The main difference is the supported browser: EPUBReader is only compatible with Mozilla Firefox.

## FILE FORMATS

A file format is a standard for encoding information to be stored in a digital file. File formats may be either proprietary or free, unpublished or open. Each file format requires software which is able to read the file.

8 Booki.sh, https://booki.sh.

9 Ebook Sales via Booki.sh to End on June 30, http://blog.booki.sh/blog/post/ebook-sales-via-booki-sh-to-end-on-june-30.

10 Readium Project Goals, http://readium.org/readium-project-goals.

11 EPUB Reader for Chrome, https://chrome.google.com/webstore/detail/readium/fepbnnnkkadjhjahcafo-aglimekefifl.

## Reflowable documents (EPUB and AZW)

The history of the modern ebook can be traced back to the late 1990s with the establishment of the Open eBook Forum, which defined a standard known as the Open eBook Publication Structure (OEBPS). This standard eventually resulted in the widely used ebook format known as EPUB, which is currently at version 3. Microsoft was heavily involved in the development of the Open eBook specification, based partly on technology developed by a company called SoftBook Press.[12] SoftBook Press originally developed the format, based on XML and XHTML, as a companion to their hardware product, which was one of the earliest dedicated e-reader devices. The Open eBook specification was first released in 1999, and later renamed EPUB for the second version release. By this time the Open eBook Forum had become the International Digital Publishing Forum (IDPF).[13] The new EPUB2 standard supported extended features such as basic styling, customized fonts, etc.[14]

When Amazon made its entrance in the world of digital publishing, the online bookseller opted not to follow the EPUB standard, but instead to purchase a French company known as Mobipocket which had developed another format called MOBI with proprietary Mobipocket Reader software that ran on some PDA (personal digital assistant) devices and other hardware.[15] One of the main reasons for this choice was the fact that, unlike EPUB, Mobipocket's products provided full support for digital rights management (DRM). ⊾ (*The Book as Directory*)

Technically, the MOBI file format is based partly on PalmDOC, an ebook file format readable on PDAs running the operating system developed by Palm, Inc., and with added support for guidelines taken from the Open eBook standard.[16] The MOBI format was further developed to be used exclusively with Mobipocket e-readers, and later with Amazon's Kindle

12 E-books: A Library on Your Lap, http://www.businessweek.com/1998/46/b3604010.htm.

13 Bläsi, C., Rothlauf, F., On the Interoperability of eBook Formats, Johannes Gutenberg-Universität Mainz, 2013, p. 12, http://wi.bwl.uni-mainz.de/publikationen/InteroperabilityReportGutenbergfinal07052013.pdf.

14 IDPF, Open Publication Structure (OPS) 2.0.1 v1.0.1, Recommended Specification September 4, 2010, 2010, http://www.idpf.org/epub/20/spec/OPS_2.0_latest.htm.

15 Rosenblatt, B., Amazon.com Acquires Mobipocket, DRMWatch.com, 2005, https://web.archive.org/web/20050426003307/http://www.drmwatch.com/drmtech/article.php/3499386.

16 PalmDOC, http://wiki.mobileread.com/wiki/PalmDOC.

e-readers. Finally, Amazon renamed the MOBI format AZW (presumably an acronym for 'Amazon Word'), which is now the generic term for all ebooks released by the company.[17]

Currently there are roughly two 'generations' of widely used ebook formats. The first generation is based on the EPUB2 standard as introduced in 2007 (or on an earlier version released under the Open eBook specification): for example, Amazon's MOBI/AZW format. The second generation usually implements features from the EPUB3 standard, while often remaining backward-compatible with older versions and subsets of EPUB2 (and to a certain extent earlier specifications as well). EPUB3, released in 2011, introduced new features such as support for HTML5 (whereas EPUB2 supported XHTML), the more advanced Cascading Style Sheets specification CSS3, scripting (which had been discouraged in EPUB2) and easy embedding of video and audio.[18] Most ebook file formats available today are based on EPUB3, including proprietary formats such as Amazon's AZW and Apple's iBooks.[19] For compatibility with older e-readers, the ebook package usually also includes a MOBI file. ⊾ (*Crash Test Dummy*)

## Other formats

The file formats described above are all reflowable documents: their presentation can be adapted for each particular output device. There are of course other ways of presenting electronic publications, for example with a fixed layout, which preserves the look of the original, including fonts, colors, images, and formatting. A common way of doing this is to export the document as a PDF, though there are also more content-specific file formats (such as 'comic book archive').[20] However, not all such formats are supported by all e-readers.

---

17 Internal Formats, http://wiki.mobileread.com/wiki/AZW#Internal_Formats.

18 EPUB3 Changes from EPUB 2.0.1, http://www.idpf.org/epub/30/spec/epub30-changes.html#sec-new-changed-xhtml5.

19 Kindle Format 8, http://www.amazon.com/gp/feature.html?ie=UTF8&docId=1000729511.

20 Comic book archive, http://fileformats.archiveteam.org/wiki/Comic_Book_Archive.

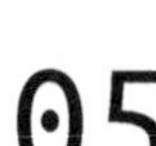

# 05

# DISTRI-BUTION PLATFORMS

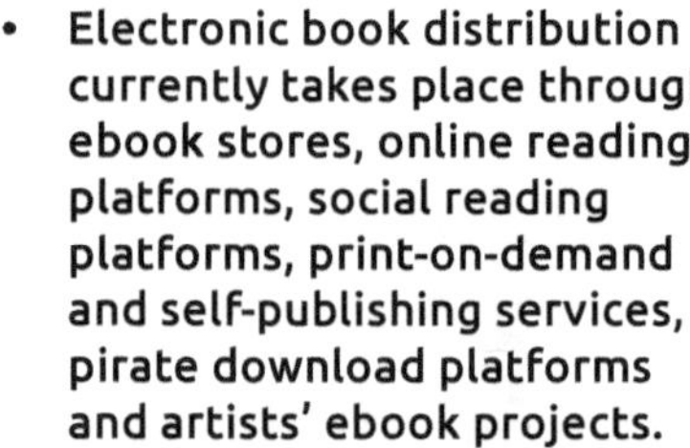

- Electronic book distribution currently takes place through ebook stores, online reading platforms, social reading platforms, print-on-demand and self-publishing services, pirate download platforms and artists' ebook projects.

- These platforms differ in their scope of content, their business strategies and the reading technologies they support.

- The choice of one or more distribution platforms therefore also determines design choices for an ebook.

## EBOOK STORES

There are many channels for the distribution of ebooks. Surprisingly, traditional retailers generally play no more than a marginal role in selling electronic publications. A notable exception is Barnes & Noble with its range of NOOK devices and dedicated ebook store. Major players in the field include Amazon, Apple, Google, Barnes & Noble and Kobo.

These ebook stores typically charge a percentage for each publication sold, usually no less than 30% of the retail price.[1,2] With the exception of Google, most of the major retailers sell their ebooks in a way that is closely integrated with their own branded e-reader hardware (Kindle, iPad, NOOK, etc.). For example, publications purchased on Amazon's Kindle are immediately downloaded to the device, rather than having to connect the device to a computer and then transfer the downloaded purchases manually.

Each retailer requires publishers to upload files in a specific format or formats. Apple for example only supports EPUB or publications made using iBooks Author, and doesn't allow PDFs.[3] Amazon with its Kindle Direct Publishing program supports a broader range of formats, including AZW, EPUB, PDF and even Microsoft Word documents.[4]

## ONLINE READING PLATFORMS

Online reading platforms are browser-based platforms for reading electronic publications. Publications can be presented in a variety of formats. The choice of online platform (and thus of publication format) also has consequences for distribution methods and accessibility. Platforms make use of a variety of business and revenue models (generating revenue for the author/publisher as well as for the platform itself) such as subscrip-

1 Apple Launches Subscriptions on the App Store, https://www.apple.com/pr/library/2011/02/15Apple-Launches-Subscriptions-on-the-App-Store.html.

2 Juliette Garside, 'Ebook sales: Amazon tells Hachette to give authors more, charge readers less', The Guardian, 30 July 2014, http://www.theguardian.com/books/2014/jul/30/amazon-hachette-ebook-sales-too-expensive.

3 Authors & Book Publishers: Frequently Asked Questions, https://www.apple.com/itunes/working-itunes/sell-content/books/book-faq.html.

4 Kindle Direct Publishing: Types of Formats, https://kdp.amazon.com/help?topicId=A2GF0UFHIYG9VQ.

tions, freemium models, consigment fees, shared revenue on sales, etc.

It is important to remember that publishers who make use of an online reading platform are effectively dependent on the platform provider. If the platform changes its technology or terms of service, or simply goes out of business, the publisher has no recourse, except possibly to find another platform. On the other hand, ebook stores which offer downloadable files provide the publisher with much more control and freedom in this respect.

The following is an overview of the main characteristics, statistics, strengths and weaknesses, revenue models and publishing guidelines for three major online reading platforms (Issuu,[5] Scribd[6] and Internet Archive[7]) as well as two third-party blogs (Medium[8] and WordPress[9]).

5 Issuu, http://www.issuu.com.

6 Scribd, http://www.scribd.com.

7 Internet Archive, https://www.archive.org.

8 Medium, https://medium.com.

9 WordPress, https://www.archive.org.

# ISSUU

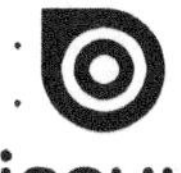

**CHARACTERISTICS**

- Books, brochures, magazines, etc.
- Allows downloading of books for offline reading
- Possible to upload a fully designed and full-color PDF
- Mostly used by independent publishers and individual users
- Supports all devices
- Supports most file formats
- Mobile and desktop
- Full embedding possibilities

**STATISTICS**

**ISSUU (JUNE 2014)**

- 80 million monthly readers
- 15 million publications

**INDIVIDUAL USERS**

- General statistics of publications
- Paid account for deeper statistics

**STRENGTHS**

- Embed on all platforms
- Sharing possibilities
- Professional look and feel
- Audio support

**WEAKNESSES**

- Publications limited to 500 pages
- No internal web store, only link to store

**REVENUE MODEL**

- Freemium model

**HOW TO PUBLISH**

- Create an account
- Upload file
- Embed on your own website
- In-screen reading with flippable pages
- Offer downloadable file

# SCRIBD

Scribd.

**CHARACTERISTICS**

- Large collection of ebooks
- For iPhone, iPad, Android, Kindle Fire, and any web browser
- Allows downloading of books for offline reading
- Supported file types: PDF, txt, ps, rtf, EPUB, key, odt, odp, ods, odg, odf, sxw, sxc, sxi, sxd, doc, ppt, pps, xls, docx, pptx, ppsx, xlsx
- Used by established publishers and for self-publishing
- Subscription model
- No limits on genre

**STATISTICS**

**SCRIBD (JUNE 2014)**
- 80 million monthly readers
- 40 million books and files
- 100 countries

**FOR INDIVIDUAL USERS**
- General statistics of publications

**STRENGTHS**

- Sharing possibilities
- Selling possibilities

**WEAKNESSES**

- Few options for metadata
- In-browser not optimal
- Embedding not optimal

**REVENUE MODEL**

- Scribd offers a subscription model for its readers and allows publishers to set a price for their work

**HOW TO PUBLISH**

- Create an account
- Upload file
- In-browser reading
- Downloadable file

# INTERNET ARCHIVE

**CHARACTERISTICS**

- Non-profit digital archive, for independent publishing
- Free public access to collections of digitized materials, including websites, ebooks, audio-visual media, software, and nearly two million public-domain books
- Free storage and access to uploaded material
- Established publishers and self-published authors
- Most text file formats are accepted (PDF, txt, rtf, EPUB, etc.)
- Texts are made available for online reading and download, in PDF, EPUB, MOBI and DjVu formats, and fully searchable

**STATISTICS**

**INTERNET ARCHIVE (OCT 2014)**
- 6 million publications
- 10 million downloads a month

**INDIVIDUAL USERS**
- Provides number of downloads of a publication

**STRENGTHS**

- Free of charge
- Easy to use
- Major ebook formats supported
- Automated conversions

**WEAKNESSES**

- No distinction between self-publishing and archival efforts
- Automated conversion errors
- Poor interface

**REVENUE MODEL**

- Uploads licensed under a Creative Commons license

**HOW TO PUBLISH**

- Create an account
- Upload publication
- Fill in publication's metadata
- The publication will be given a dedicated page

# LULU

## CHARACTERISTICS

- Lulu is the biggest print-on-demand service which offers publishing free of cost, based on a model of shared profit
- Available in six languages: English, French, Spanish, German, Italian and Dutch
- Used in 225 countries and territories; 1.8 million publications; 20,000 new publications each month
- 1.1 million authors
- Mostly for self-publishing
- Mostly for publishing books
- Lulu also offers an ebook publishing service

## STRENGTHS

- Ability to set your own price
- Possible distribution through Amazon, Barnes & Noble, and Apple's iBookstore (ebooks only)
- Free ISBN available

## WEAKNESSES

- Prices can vary considerably even for the same publication, particularly due to postal costs
- Minimum and maximum number of pages
- Only a number of specific print dimensions (width x height) are allowed
- Interface and help section are not very user-friendly

## REVENUE MODEL

- Authors/publishers get 80% of the profit of a publication, Lulu gets 20%

## HOW TO PRINT

- Create an account
- You will need two PDFs: one for the cover and spine, another for the rest of the book
- Choose your format, paper, etc.
- You can provide your own ISBN number, or have Lulu assign an ISBN
- If you don't have a cover yet, you can use a browser-based editor to design one
- Upload the PDFs and publish your work
- Choose your preferred methods of distribution

# MEDIUM

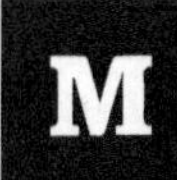

**CHARACTERISTICS**

- External party
- Text-based
- Not for publishing whole books, but e.g. a summary or chapter
- Strong connection with social media such as Twitter and Facebook

**STATISTICS**

- Medium offers statistics for individual users, including referrers

**STRENGTHS**

- New audiences & communities
- Easy to use
- Designed for reading
- Responsive website

**WEAKNESSES**

- Third-party website
- Suitable for shorter texts only
- Login with Twitter or Facebook only

**REVENUE MODEL**

- Medium has an editorial staff, getting paid per click
- There is no revenue model for individual, external users

**HOW TO PUBLISH**

- Create an account and upload text for blog

# WORDPRESS

## CHARACTERISTICS

- External party
- Mainly used for text
- Not for publishing whole books, but e.g. excerpts or blogs

## STATISTICS

- WordPress provides stats for individual users, including referrers

## STRENGTHS

- Open Source
- Free
- Easy to use
- Designed for reading
- Mobile and desktop
- Options for digital publishing through plug-ins

## WEAKNESSES

- Third-party website
- Suitable for shorter texts only

## REVENUE MODEL

- Wordpress can easily be used to make a web store

## HOW TO PUBLISH

- Create an account
- Upload text for blog

# ESPRESSO BOOK MACHINE

## CHARACTERISTICS

- The Espresso Book Machine (EBM) is a direct-to-consumer print-on-demand machine that prints, collates, covers, and binds a single copy of a book in a few minutes; it can be found at different locations, for example in physical bookstores
- Input is PDF
- A book can be stored in a database, allowing other customers at other locations to purchase a copy
- Can also print copyright-free books from Google Books
- Price is roughly equivalent to that of a regular book

## STRENGTHS

- Print as few or as many copies as desired
- The book is immediately printed on the spot
- Green technology

## WEAKNESSES

- The Espresso Book Machine is tied to a location and for now mostly available across the United States, with two locations in the Netherlands (American Book Center in Amsterdam and The Hague), and various other locations worldwide
- Options vary per location
- Limitations in paper, color, size

## REVENUE MODEL

- The bookstore where the Espresso Book Machine is located gets a small consignment fee for each printed book; self-publishers can set their own price

## HOW TO PRINT

- You will need two PDFs: one for the cover and spine, another for the rest of the book
- Sign the affidavit stating you own the rights to the book
- Choose your preferred methods of distribution

### Social reading platforms

Social reading, a combination of social networking and reading ebooks, is a relatively new phenomenon with much potential for future developments. A detailed discussion of the topic would lead us beyond the scope of this Toolkit; however, publishers working on electronic publications are advised to keep an eye on developments in social reading. Examples of social reading platforms:

- Goodreads – 'Goodreads is the world's largest site for readers and book recommendations. Our mission is to help people find and share books they love. Goodreads launched in January 2007.'
- Social Book – 'Social Book, created by the Institute for the Future of the Book, is a social reading platform that allows readers to add their own commentary to texts, share these ideas with others, follow others' comments, and create communities of interactive readers/writers.'
- Wattpad – 'Wattpad stories are free. Whether you're online or off, use the devices you already own to carry an entire library wherever you go [...] Join the conversation about the stories you read: message the writer and interact with other people who love the story as much as you.'
- Hebban – A Dutch social reading platform.
- Discussions on social media are also part of the social reading experience: Twitter interviews, Facebook pages for newly released books, book reviews in podcasts or on YouTube.

## PRINT-ON-DEMAND (POD)

There are many services which offer print-on-demand publishing; a simple Google search for the term will turn up a myriad of results. The following section is a brief description of the most important services, in the Netherlands as well as abroad. Of course many 'regular' printers also offer print-on-demand services, though they usually require a minimum number of copies to be printed. The following is an overview of the main characteristics, strengths and weaknesses, revenue models and publishing guidelines for two major print-on-demand services, Lulu[10] and the Espresso Book Machine.[11]

10 Lulu, https://www.lulu.com.

11 Espresso Book Machine, http://www.ondemandbooks.com/.

## International options

- Kobo Writing Life[12] – Allows authors and publishers to self-publish digital content in 160+ countries. The Kobo Writing Life website can be used to publish ebooks and to track sales.
- PubIt![13] – Automatically converts digital files for viewing on NOOK, mobile, and computing devices. Also helps authors and publishers distribute their ebooks.
- Smashwords[14] – Makes it free and easy to publish, distribute and sell ebooks globally through the largest ebook retailers, including Apple's iBookstore, Barnes & Noble, Sony, Kobo, Baker & Taylor, Diesel eBooks and more. There are no setup fees and no extra costs for updating or revising a published book.
- XinXii[15] – Allows authors to upload and sell their publications online on their XinXii author page: short works, documents and ebooks, in multiple formats including PDF, EPUB and MOBI, as well as audiobooks. As an aggregator, XinXii distributes to major international ebook retailers.

## Options in the Netherlands

- CB's print-on-demand service[16] – The largest Dutch supplier of non-specialist printed books to bookstores and consumers. In addition to selling ebooks through Dutch and Belgian retailers, CB also facilitates international sales. One of the services offered is print-on-demand. This is directed primarily at publishers already working with the CB distribution center. The book will remain available through the databases used by bookstores and publishers, in the same way as paper books.
- Boekscout[17] – Is one of the main print-on-demand publishers in the Netherlands, focused on self-publishing.

---

12 Kobo Writing Life is where it all begins, http://www.kobobooks.com/kobowritinglife.

13 Self-Publishing Made Simple, http://pubit.barnesandnoble.com/.

14 How to Create, Publish, and Distribute Ebooks with Smashwords, http://www.smashwords.com/about/how_to_publish_on_smashwords.

15 Xin Xii, http://www.xinxii.com/.

16 CB print-on-demand, http://www.cb-logistics.nl/markten/media/uitgeverijen/logistieke-diensten/print-on-demand/.

17 Boekscout, http://www.boekscout.nl/.

## PIRATE PLATFORMS: THE PIRATE BAY, LIBRARY.RU, AAAAARG, MONOSKOP

As with music and films, 'pirate' platforms haven often been at the avant-garde of electronic publishing. They provide music, films, games and electronic books as free downloads – either in outright violation of copyrights, or in legal 'gray zones' (obscure and out-of-print books, films or recordings of which the rights owners are unknown). The mere existence and popularity of pirate sites for digitized books is in itself an indication of the actual size of the market for electronic reading. Pirate platforms are, by their nature, more volatile than online bookstores and e-reading platforms. Worldwide there are various organizations dedicated to fighting piracy and shutting down pirate websites, even small-scale ones. However pirate platforms have usually proven quite resilient to such crackdown attempts by copyright enforcers, often reincarnating on a different web domain shortly after a forced closure.

Commercial providers of digital content can (and do) learn a lot from pirate platforms. For example, Netflix,[18] the most successful web service for streaming films and a growing competitor to paid cable television, has been known to decide which films to show based on the popularity of these films on The Pirate Bay.[19]

### All-purpose download sites

Sites like The Pirate Bay offer every imaginable type of digital media for download: films, music, computer games and software, and of course electronic books. The content listed on The Pirate Bay (and other sites which make use of the file-sharing protocol known as BitTorrent) tends toward the mainstream: Hollywood films, pop music, and non-fiction and technical handbook literature as well as fantasy and science fiction. Since these sites are widely used and provide up-to-date download statistics, and since their technology (BitTorrent) depends on user participation for downloads to remain available, they provide a great deal of insight into which titles are truly popular among readers, as well as the popularity of ebooks in general. For example, at a particular moment in June 2014, the book *Atlas of Ancient Worlds*

18 Netflix, http://www.netflix.com.

19 The Pirate Bay, http://thepiratebay.se.

had been downloaded more than 2000 times in 48 hours (in comparison, the most popular film – an episode of the TV series *Game of Thrones* – had been downloaded more than 70,000 times).

### General ebook sites

Besides sites such as Project Gutenberg,[20] where users can legally download copyright-free ebooks, there are many websites where ebooks are shared illegally. The most simple ebook pirate sites offer every kind of book – very much like a large general-audience bookstore or Amazon's online bookstores. This type of site, which is in fact little more than a simple search engine with downloadable content such as ebooks, is particularly popular in Russia. At the time of writing, library.ru was the model for this type of site. After its forced closure, the vacuum was soon filled by other sites such as bookfi.org.[21] Another example worth mentioning here is the online library libgen.info.[22]

### Specialized sites

Some websites which operate outside (or in 'gray zones') of copyright law are in fact art projects. In the 1990s the website 'textz.com', created by the Berlin-based artist Sebastian Luetgert, was the first website to offer books on culture, politics and media theory as simple, freely downloadable text files (incidentally, the name 'textz' was a pun on 'warez', a slang term for illegally copied software). Later, other websites such as AAAAARG[23] and Monoskop[24] provided thematically linked collections of freely downloadable books on art, culture and media studies, with the stated goal of stimulating reading and discussion groups, or of offering a carefully hand-selected library according to the specific tastes of the website's owner.

---

20 Project Gutenberg, http://www.gutenberg.org/.

21 Bookfi.org, http://bookfi.org.

22 Libgen.info, http://libgen.info.

23 AAAAARG, http://aaaaarg.org/.

24 Monoskop Log, http://monoskop.org/log.

The most well-known of these is UbuWeb,[25] a website offering an encyclopedic scope of downloadable audio, video and plain-text versions of avant-garde art recordings, films and books. Most of the books fall in the category of small-edition artists' books and are presented here with the permission of the artists in question, who are not so concerned with potential loss of revenue since most of the works are officially out of print and never made any money even when they were commercially available.

All these websites are operated much like small specialized bookstores – even though they don't sell anything. However they demonstrate the viability of an approach which is the complete opposite of that of mainstream businesses such as Amazon and bookfi.org – namely, offering a relatively small collection of personally selected publications. If the website enjoys a strong reputation, as in the case of UbuWeb, AAAAARG or Monoskop, users will regularly return to the site, and download and read works by authors they have never even heard of, simply based on the fact that the work is available on a site they trust.

What online booksellers could learn from these websites:

- Simplicity combined with encyclopedic scope. No other website except Amazon makes it so easy to find and download electronic books in any genre or language, from bestsellers to obscure out-of-print cult classics.
- Simplicity of format. The sites provide mostly PDFs and EPUBs, depending on the format the work was presented in.

## ARTIST AND DESIGNER-RUN PROJECTS: BADLANDS UNLIMITED, KYUR8, ARTISTSEBOOKS.ORG

In recent years there have been efforts to set up small presses and book download stores focusing exclusively on artists' and designers' books: for example the writer, artist and publisher James Bridle (who coined the term 'new aesthetics') created *Artists' eBooks*, a website featuring freely download-

25 UbuWeb, http://www.ubu.com .

able EPUB files by experimental writers and artists.[26] Another example is the more commercially oriented online press Badlands Unlimited, an initiative of the American contemporary artist and designer Paul Chan, which sells artist-made visual electronic books, available only in Apple's proprietary format for the iPad tablet and iBooks platform.

The iPhone/iPad app KYUR8 ('curate') invites artists to quickly assemble their own electronic visual magazine using page templates and photo collections taken from the user's cell phone. Other examples include gauss-pdf.com, a publisher of digital and printed works and trollthread.tumblr.com, a collective of poets with publications available for download in PDF or for purchase through print-on-demand.

Of course, none of these projects can be considered serious competition to mainstream ebook stores, online reading platforms or even specialist pirate websites since they are, after all, experimental projects and artists' portfolio pieces.

26 Artists' eBooks, http://artistsebook.org.

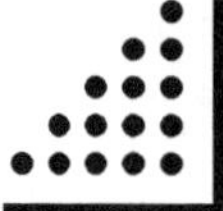

# 06

# GUIDE: HOW TO MAKE A SIMPLE EPUB

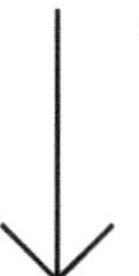

- An EPUB file can be seen as a self-contained website with some metadata files, packed together in a zip archive.
- EPUBs can be created from scratch, with any text editor, simply by creating some HTML files and the required metadata files, and placing all these files inside specific folders.
- EPUBs can also be exported from InDesign projects, provided the workflow within InDesign is done in a highly structured way, and preferably using the very latest version of the software.
- The Open Source command-line program Pandoc is a powerful tool for converting various types of text-based files into EPUB. However, the quality of the converted document is highly dependent on the degree to which the markup of the input file is well-structured.
- The Open Source software Calibre, which features a graphical user interface (GUI), can alternatively be used for document conversion and editing.

Making an EPUB doesn't have to be a complicated process. Since the EPUB standard is open and based on HTML (the same standard used for designing web pages), there's an increasingly large number of ways of converting and exporting different types of source file formats to EPUB. For very simple publications, it may be possible to use a software tool that directly converts your document to EPUB. However, before exploring in detail any of these do-it-yourself tools, we will first explain what an EPUB contains, how it works, and how to make one from scratch.

This chapter consists of four sections:

1. Do-it-yourself EPUB from scratch
2. Do-it-yourself EPUB using InDesign
3. Do-it-yourself EPUB using Pandoc
4. Using Calibre and custom plug-ins

## DO-IT-YOURSELF EPUB FROM SCRATCH

The process of creating an EPUB from scratch is similar to that of developing a simple website. The main difference is that while websites can and often do embed material located elsewhere on the internet, an EPUB is 'self-contained' and made for offline reading. This means that all pages or images displayed must be part of the collection. Making an EPUB from scratch, or manually, is useful for creating small and simple publications, for creating or modifying publications that make extensive use of the particularities of the EPUB format, or in order to explore and better understand the functionalities and inner workings of this format, which is what we will now do.

An EPUB file is in fact a ZIP archive, but with the filename extension '.epub' instead of '.zip'. As such, it is a compressed collection of HTML files, style sheets and images, much like the files found on a website, compiled together with some extra files which define the format and structure of the documents so that an e-reader can display them. Any file archiving software that can handle ZIP files can open and decompress an EPUB. In some cases this can be done simply by renaming the '.epub' extension to '.zip'.[1]

1 More information on how to automate the EPUB zipping process can be found here: EPUB Zip/Unzip AppleScript application for Mac OS X, http://www.mobileread.com/forums/showthread.php?t=55681.

For a better understanding of the following explanation of what an EPUB is and how to create one, we suggest downloading a working example of a rudimentary EPUB, which can be found on Toolkit project's GitHub page (a direct link can be found in the footnote).[2]

### Structure of an EPUB package

Decompressing an EPUB file will reveal its internal folder (or directory) structure. Examining this structure will help us understand how an EPUB is put together. As explained above, the EPUB is a compressed ZIP archive. Start by decompressing or 'unzipping' the EPUB file using the built-in archive utility of your computer operating system, or archiving/compression software such as The Unarchiver (Mac), WinZip (Windows), etc. The unzipped contents should look like this:

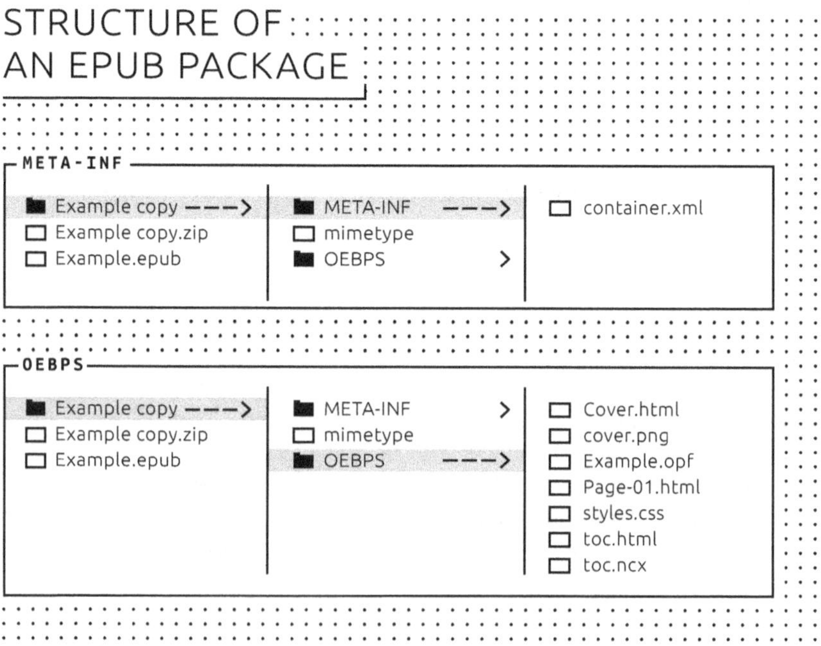

STRUCTURE OF AN EPUB PACKAGE



2 Example EPUB, https://github.com/DigitalPublishingToolkit/Hybrid-Publishing-Toolkit-for-the-Arts/raw/master/examples/Example.epub.

The *META-INF* and *OEBPS* directories and the *mimetype* file are required components, and are an important part of what constitutes an EPUB:

- The *META-INF* folder contains an XML file (*container.xml*) which directs the e-reader device or application to an inventory (an .opf file) of all the files used by the publication.
- The *OEBPS* folder is the location where all of the publication's content (HTML files, images, audio, video, etc.) is stored; subdirectories are allowed but not mandatory. The .opf file (traditionally named *content.opf*) is a key component; this file contains the metadata for the EPUB, and is in turn referenced by the aforementioned *container.xml* file. You may also see another file with a .ncx extension (traditionally *toc.ncx*), which contains the hierarchical table of contents for the EPUB, however this file is optional as it is not part of the EPUB specification.
- *Mimetype* is a file which contains a single line describing the EPUB file as 'application/epub+zip'; this file allows e-readers to check whether the file is actually an EPUB which they can read.

These three components form the basic structure of an EPUB, and are required in order for the file to be a valid EPUB.[3]

## Creating your own EPUB

Most of the elements of an EPUB can be manually typed in a text editor. Text editors are used for editing plain-text files such as HTML files, and should not to be confused with word processors such as Microsoft Word or Apple's Pages (though it is of course entirely possible to create and edit text plain-files using a word processor). Popular text editors include BBEdit, TextWrangler or TextMate for Mac, or NotePad++ and PSPad for Windows. The following is a step-by-step description of the process of creating a very simple EPUB.

3 The following overview at idpf.org defines the semantics and conformance requirements for EPUB publications: EPUB Publications 3.0.1. Recommended Specification 26 June 2014, http://www.idpf.org/epub/301/spec/epub-publications.html.

### Creating the required files and directories

Now that we've seen the internal structure of an EPUB by unzipping it, we can also work the other way round and make the files and directories ourselves, thus creating a simple EPUB. We will work from our *Documents* folder where we will add subdirectories as in the image above, and create the necessary files using a text editor.

1. Create a subfolder in the *Documents* folder and name it *Example*.
2. Create two more subdirectories under the one you've just created, one called *META-INF* and the other called *OEBPS*.
3. Using a text editor, create a plain-text file and type (or copy-paste) the line 'application/epub+zip' (without quotation marks) in this file.
4. Save this plain-text file and name it *mimetype* (without a filename extension). Save it in the same folder (named *Example*) as the two subdirectories created in step 2. This way the e-reader device or application can see that these elements together constitute an EPUB.

Now there are the two directories and one text file, just as we saw when we decompressed the EPUB which we used as an example.

### container.xml

Next we will create the file *container.xml*, the XML file (located in the *META-INF* folder) that directs the e-reader device or application to an inventory of all the files present in the publication.

1. Again using a text editor, create a new plain-text file and save it to the *META-INF* folder with the name *container.xml*.
2. The file *container.xml* contains a simple structure definition written in XML. Below is a complete version of the XML, followed by an explanation of its separate components. (The technical explanations are not essential to understanding the text and may be skipped.)

```
<?xml version="1.0" encoding="UTF-8"?>
<container version="1.0" xmlns="urn:oasis:names:tc:opendocu-
ment:xmlns:container">
  <rootfiles>
  <rootfile full-path="OEBPS/content.opf" media-type="application/
oebps-package+xml"/>
  </rootfiles>
</container>
```

The first line is a declaration statement, which should always be present in XML files. This is followed by a 'container' tag indicating that the publication is based on the Open Container Format as specified by the EPUB standard.[4] Next, the 'rootfiles' tag indicates a collection of rootfiles: these are the possible starting points where the e-reader can begin processing the content. In this case the rootfiles statement contains only one entry, called 'rootfile'; this tag has two attributes, 'full-path' and 'media-type'. The first attribute is the path to an inventory file (in this case *content.opf*) containing metadata describing the publication and its content. Finally, 'media-type' is a restatement of the EPUB's mimetype.

The most important part of this document is the information in quotes following the 'full-path' attribute: 'OEBPS/content.opf'. This attribute should indicate the name of an .opf file which we will create in the next step.

3. Save and close the text file *container.xml*.

**The .opf file**

The .opf (Open Packaging Format) file is an important part of the structure of an EPUB. It is located in the *OEBPS* folder and contains the metadata necessary to accurately describe the publication. It can also contain the linear reading order which, in combination with the contents of *toc.ncx*, may be used by e-readers to build navigation menus or a table of contents. The .opf file is too long to be included verbatim in the present document, but the most important sections are referenced below. An example of a complete .opf file can be found in the rudimentary example EPUB, in the *OEBPS* folder and under the name *Example.opf*.

```
<metadata xmlns:dc="http://purl.org/dc/elements/1.1/"
  xmlns:opf="http://www.idpf.org/2007/opf"
  xmlns:xsi="http://www.w3.org/2001/XMLSchema-instance">
  <dc:title>Example EPUB</dc:title>
  <dc:language>en</dc:language>
  <dc:identifier id="BookId">http://digitalpublishingtoolkit.org/Exam-
  pleEPUB.html</dc:identifier>
  <meta property="dcterms:modified">2014-03-28T14:11:50Z</meta>
  ...
</metadata>
```

4 EPUB Open Container Format (OCF) 3.0, http://www.idpf.org/epub/30/spec/epub30-ocf.html.

The 'metadata' section contains a description of the publication: title, author, publisher, etc. Most of these entries are identical to what librarians use for cataloguing publications. Parts of the metadata section are used by e-readers to organize ebook collections.

```
<manifest>
   <item href="styles.css" id="css1" media-type="text/css"/>
   <item href="cover.png" id="cover" media-type="image/png" proper-
   ties="cover-image"/>
   <item id="chapter1" href="Cover.html" media-type="application/
   xhtml+xml" />
   <item id="chapter2" href="Page-01.html" media-type="application/
   xhtml+xml" />
   <item properties="nav" id="toc" href="toc.html" media-type="appli-
   cation/xhtml+xml" />
   <item href="toc.ncx" id="ncx" media-type="application/x-dtbncx-
   +xml"/>
</manifest>
```

The 'manifest' section lists all the resources used in the EPUB package, with the exception of subdirectories, the *mimetype* file, the contents of the *META-INF* folder, and the .opf file itself. Manually producing a manifest section can be extremely time-consuming for large EPUBs, as the list of resources used in the publication is bound to be long. Every resource has a unique 'id' and should be referenced by a relative path in the 'href' attribute and described in the 'media-type' attribute. The entry with the *cover.png* is of special interest, as its 'properties' attribute specifies that the image may be used by e-readers as a cover image for the publication, for example in collection overviews.

```
<spine toc="ncx">
   <itemref idref="chapter1" />
   <itemref idref="chapter2" />
</spine>
```

Finally, the 'spine' section lists all the HTML or XHTML pages present in the publication; the order of this list indicates to the e-reader the linear reading order of the publication. The 'spine' section contains only HTML or XHTML pages, no images or other content. The 'toc' attribute refers to the 'id' attribute of the 'toc.ncx' file already described in the 'manifest' section.

### The content

As mentioned in the introduction of this section, an important part of an EPUB consists of a collection of HTML files, often connected through hyperlinks. The process of creating the pages of an EPUB is similar to that of building a website, but with the particular limitations of e-readers in mind – limited support for rich media, color, etc. (see also Chapter 4: Technologies for electronic reading Pages should be written in XHTML, a variant of HTML that was created to make HTML more 'extensible' and increase its interoperability with other data formats. Cascading Style Sheets (CSS) may freely be used, although many e-readers will ignore at least some of the style definitions.

### Packaging

Putting together the EPUB file is quite simple: select the *META-INF* and *OEBPS* directories together with the *mimetype* file, and create a ZIP archive. This may be done by using the built-in archive utility of your computer operating system, or an external program or utility.[5] The .zip extension of the archive must then be renamed to .epub.

Because some archive programs create unnecessary (hidden) files inside the archive which might make your EPUB invalid, it's important to 'validate' your EPUB to see if it actually works (although in practice, most e-readers will safely ignore superfluous files and still interpret the document properly). Invalid EPUBs are files that do not conform to the EPUB specification, or have other issues such as incorrect code. Fixing validation errors will minimize (but not eliminate) the chance of e-readers refusing to read an EPUB. Validation of the EPUB can be done online using the EPUB Validator[6] or with a specialized desktop application.

---

**And your EPUB is ready!**

5 More information on how to automate the EPUB zipping process can be found here: EPUB Zip/Unzip AppleScript application for Mac OS X, http://www.mobileread.com/forums/showthread.php?t=55681.

6 EPUB Validator (beta), http://validator.idpf.org.

## DO-IT-YOURSELF EPUB USING INDESIGN

InDesign is an excellent tool for creating and managing print projects. It also includes a powerful EPUB production tool which has steadily improved over time. InDesign's omnipresence and importance in print design make it an obvious choice for projects that have both print and electronic outputs. InDesign is so powerful that it will be useful even if print isn't part of the equation – though cost considerations may preclude its use if print is not going to be a requirement. Below we will describe step-by-step how to create an EPUB with custom layout using InDesign.

Another option when using InDesign is to import files in the ICML file format. There are a number of tools for converting text files from various formats to ICML. The files can then be used to create print PDFs and EPUBs from the same InDesign document. For a step-by-step description of this process, please go to the Toolkit blog. ⊾ (*Markdown to InDesign with Pandoc (via ICML)*)

InDesign can generate both reflowable and fixed-layout EPUB files. Reflowable layout means that the size and positioning of text and images are adjusted according to the screen size as well as the user's individual preferences. Fixed layout means that the text and images are always shown in the same (relative) size and positions on a page, regardless of the screen size or other factors. Fixed-layout text and images are usually reduced in size to fit on smaller screens, often to the point of becoming completely illegible on mobile phones. Finally, reflowable EPUB is supported by a broader range of e-readers and tablets, while fixed layout is supported by only a few.

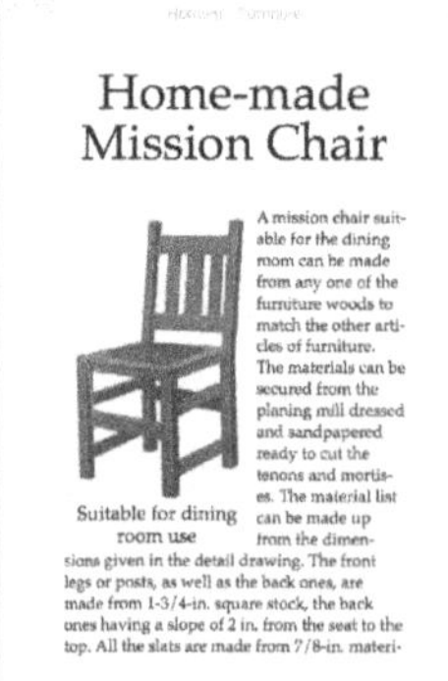

Home-made Mission Chair

Suitable for dining room use

A mission chair suitable for the dining room can be made from any one of the furniture woods to match the other articles of furniture. The materials can be secured from the planing mill dressed and sandpapered ready to cut the tenons and mortises. The material list can be made up from the dimensions given in the detail drawing. The front legs or posts, as well as the back ones, are made from 1-3/4-in. square stock, the back ones having a slope of 2 in. from the seat to the top. All the slats are made from 7/8-in. materi-

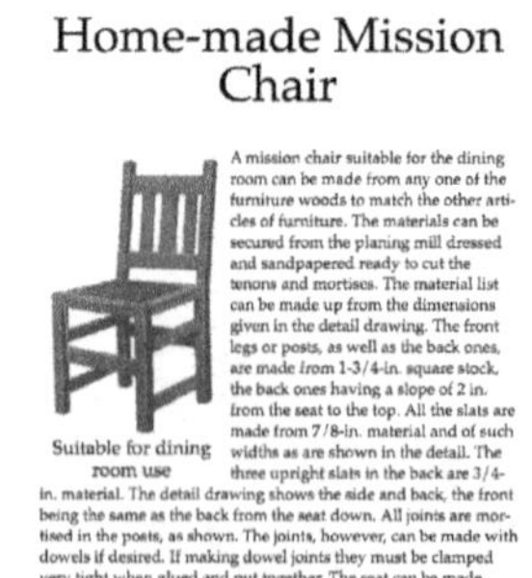

Home-made Mission Chair

Suitable for dining room use

A mission chair suitable for the dining room can be made from any one of the furniture woods to match the other articles of furniture. The materials can be secured from the planing mill dressed and sandpapered ready to cut the tenons and mortises. The material list can be made up from the dimensions given in the detail drawing. The front legs or posts, as well as the back ones, are made from 1-3/4-in. square stock, the back ones having a slope of 2 in. from the seat to the top. All the slats are made from 7/8-in. material and of such widths as are shown in the detail. The three upright slats in the back are 3/4-in. material. The detail drawing shows the side and back, the front being the same as the back from the seat down. All joints are mortised in the posts, as shown. The joints, however, can be made with dowels if desired. If making dowel joints they must be clamped very tight when glued and put together. The seat can be made

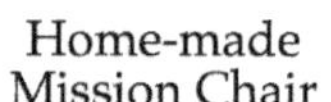

Home-made Mission Chair

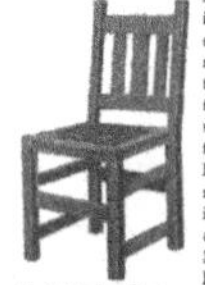

Suitable for dining room use

A mission chair suitable for the dining room can be made from any one of the furniture woods to match the other articles of furniture. The materials can be secured from the planing mill dressed and sandpapered ready to cut the tenons and mortises. The material list can be made up from the dimensions given in the detail drawing. The front legs or posts, as well as the back ones, are made from 1-3/4-in. square stock, the back ones having a slope of 2 in. from the seat to the top. All the slats are made from 7/8-in. material and of such widths as are shown in the detail. The three upright slats in the back are 3/4-in. material. The detail drawing shows the side and back, the front being the same as the back from the seat down. All joints are mortised in the posts, as shown. The joints, however, can be made with dowels if desired. If mak-

InDesign's features for print layouts – such as master pages, control of headers and footers, and precise positioning of text, images and other elements – are ignored in reflowable EPUB documents. However reflowable EPUB does permit choosing settings such as (initial) font size, leading, font type, spacing before and after paragraphs, whether a paragraph should begin on a new page, etc. Keep in mind however that individual users are often able to partially or completely override these settings in their e-reader devices or applications.

InDesign can also be used purely for EPUB production, with no print output. In this case you can simply ignore how the book looks in print, and focus instead on generating flexible EPUB documents that look good and work well across a range of e-readers.

The most important thing when creating EPUBs using InDesign (or any other tool for that matter) is to make sure that the layout of the documents you are working with is as structured as possible. Therefore we will begin this guide by applying structured formatting (known as 'styles') to the various elements of the manuscript.

Keep in mind that this is a very brief step-by-step guide, while InDesign is a very complex general-purpose software package with many more options than those described here.

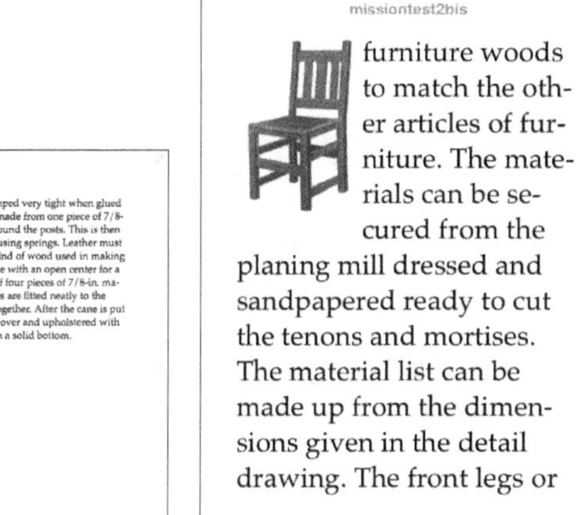


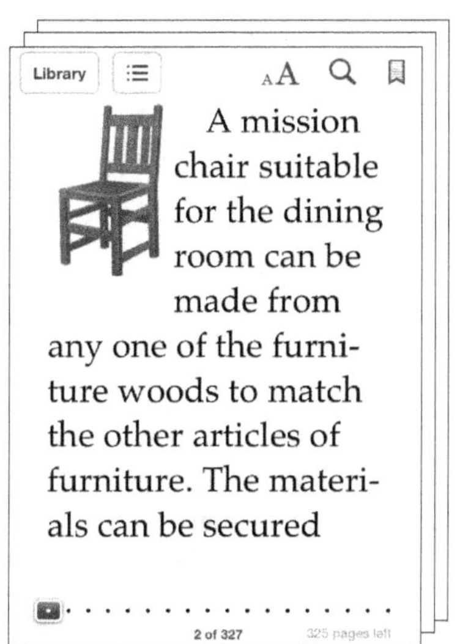

## Styles

One of the most powerful tools provided by InDesign is the ability to identify different kinds of paragraphs (headings, sub-headings, body text, captions, etc.) and to instantly apply a whole set of formatting rules to such a group of paragraphs. Each defined set of rules is called a 'style'. These styles can later be exported to the EPUB in Cascading Style Sheets (CSS) format, allowing for any subsequent editing and adjustments which may be necessary in order to adapt the EPUB to a range of different devices, and/or to define layout settings for the EPUB which are different from those in the print document. First we must define the styles, then apply them, and finally make sure they are properly mapped for export to EPUB.

Creating styles

1. To create a new style, open the Paragraph Styles panel (accessed through Type > Paragraph Styles) and select New Paragraph Style from the panel menu (panel menus are accessed by clicking the icon in the upper right-hand corner). Any formatting in the active paragraph will be incorporated automatically into the new style.
2. Give the style a name.
3. Select any additional options. The right-hand side of the dialog box will show different options, depending on the category selected on the left-hand side.

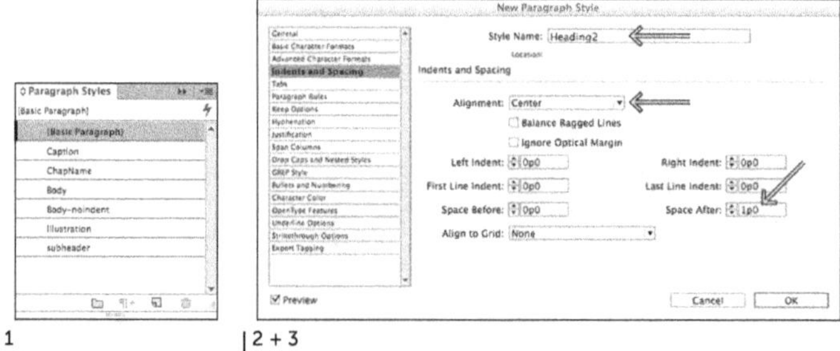


1 2 + 3

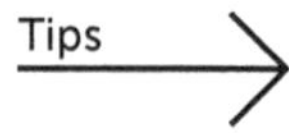


- **Besides paragraph styles, you can also create character styles, which apply formatting to a selection of text rather than an entire paragraph.**
- **Using defined styles rather than directly applying formatting improves reliability across e-readers and makes later editing and updating of the layout much easier and more consistent.**

Applying styles

1. Click anywhere in the paragraph to which you want to apply the style.
2. Choose the desired style from the Paragraph Styles panel.
3. Repeat steps 1 and 2 for all paragraphs in the document.

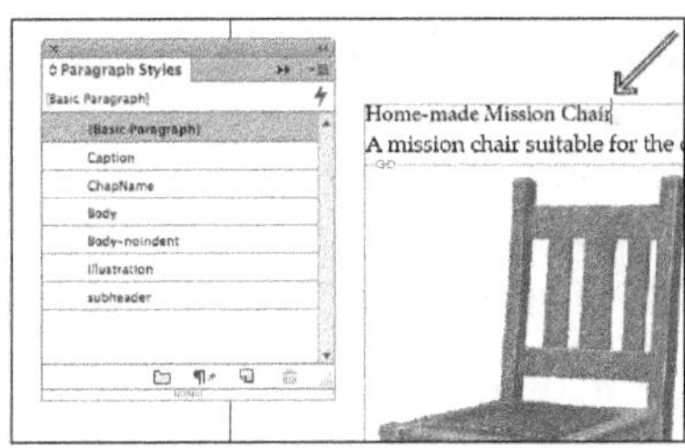


1

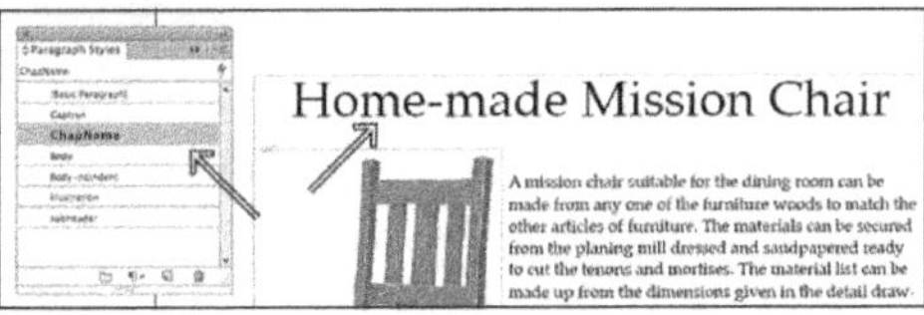


2

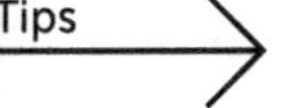
Tips

- **You can apply a basic style to all paragraphs at once by choosing Select All and then choosing a basic style such as Body or Normal, after which you can individually apply the less frequent heading, caption and other paragraph styles to the relevant paragraphs.**
- **If you have imported a document with large quantities of existing bold or italic text, you can automatically apply a character style using the search and replace function.***

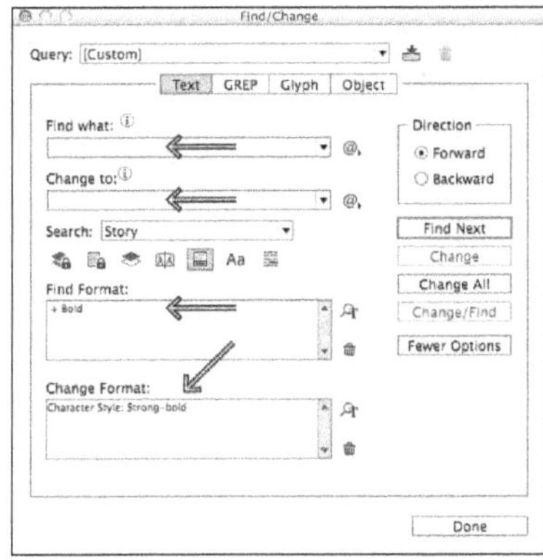


*

### Mapping styles to tags

Though InDesign can perform this step automatically, for more control you can specify exactly which Paragraph Styles should be mapped to which tags in the resulting CSS.

1. Choose Edit All Export Tags from the Paragraph Styles panel menu.
2. In the dialog box that appears, verify that each style in the Style column is mapped to the appropriate CSS in the Tag column. It's a good idea, for example, for heading paragraphs in your book to be exported as 'h1', 'h2', etc., and also for each style to have its own 'Class'.

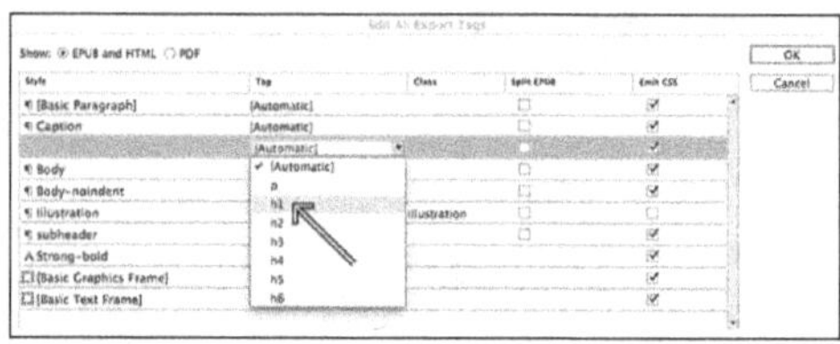


1 + 2

Tips

- **If you import XML documents, you can have InDesign automatically map specific XML tags to the desired paragraph styles (which later will be mapped to the proper EPUB CSS tags).**
- **You can also map a style to a tag by selecting Export Tagging in the Paragraph Style and Character Style dialog boxes.**
- **Earlier versions of InDesign were not so good at exporting all of a document's styles to CSS. The most recent version InDesign CC offers a substantial improvement in this respect.***
- **Besides (or in addition to) the formatting from the styles provided by InDesign, you can apply your own CSS in the 'EPUB – Reflowable Layout Export Options' dialog box (see the Export Options section of this step-by-step guide).**

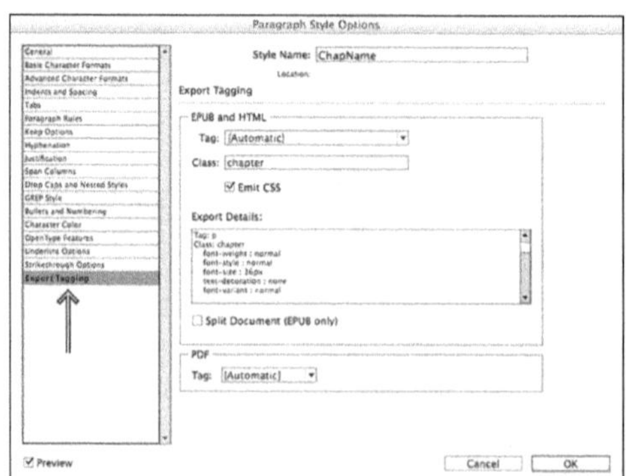


*

## Images

InDesign places images in the layout in one of three ways: inline, anchored or independent:

- Inline images are placed or pasted directly in the text. When exported, they are rasterized (rendered as pixels or dots); thus if any inline object contains text, this text will also be rasterized. The image is then included in the flow of the text in which it was placed. Inline images cannot have text wrapped around them.
- Anchored images are linked to a particular location in the text, known as an anchor; when exported to EPUB they will appear at that location. Anchored images may have text wrapped around them, and are exported as floating objects in an EPUB. Text contained in anchored objects is not rasterized. However it will sometimes be resized incorrectly by the e-reader device or application.
- Independent images are placed alongside text and other objects, without any explicit link between the two. InDesign exports text and independent image objects sequentially according to their location on the page, from the top down and from left to right. Since an entire text flow is exported before any other objects on the same page, independent images may appear much further in the EPUB than they did in the print version. The order of exported objects can be adjusted in the Articles panel (accessed through Window > Articles).

### Anchoring images

Generally it's a good idea to use anchored images for a layout that will be exported to EPUB. This gives you more control over where the image appears in the exported EPUB, and also allows the text to wrap around the image.

1. Place an image on the pasteboard.
2. If desired, you can create a caption, apply a style to the caption, and then group the caption with the image.
3. Select the image in order to make its controls visible. Click and drag the blue box (near the upper right-hand corner of the image) to the desired location in the text. The blue box now changes to an anchor symbol.
4. If the layout of the print output is important, adjust the location of the image. This does not affect the image's location in the EPUB.
5. If you want the text to wrap around the image, select the image and then choose Object > Object Export Options.

a. Select the 'EPUB and HTML' options tab.
b. Check the Custom Layout check box, and choose Float Left or Float Right from the pull-down menu.
c. To specify the amount of space between the image and the text, select the image, display the Text Wrap dialog box, click the second icon from the left, and specify the amount of space above, below, left and right in each field.

You can also use this option to adjust how the image appears in the print edition.

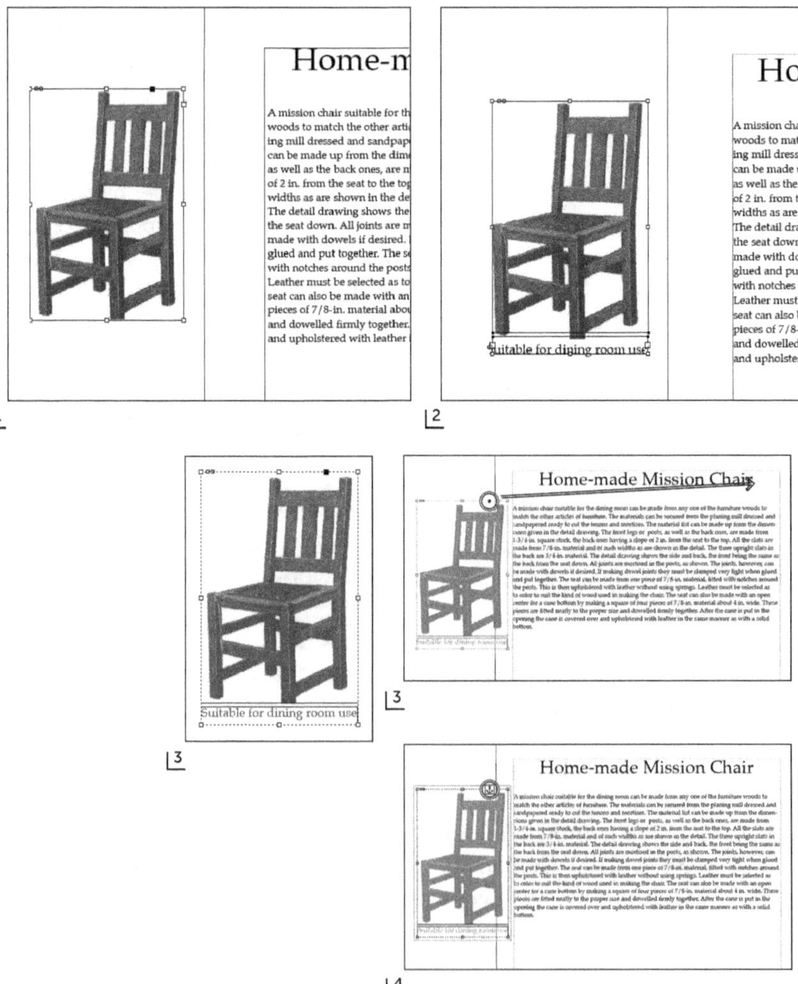

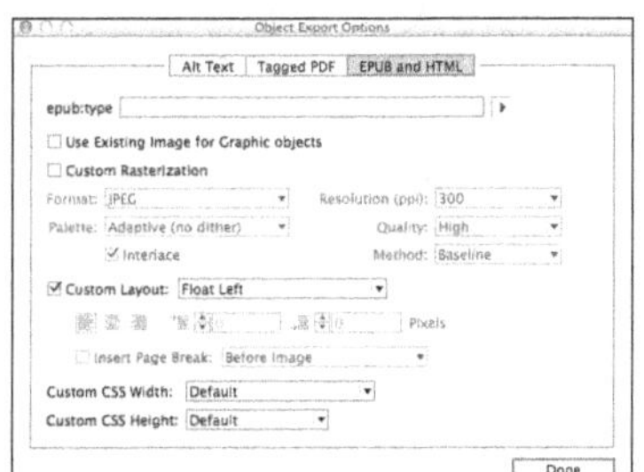


5 a + b

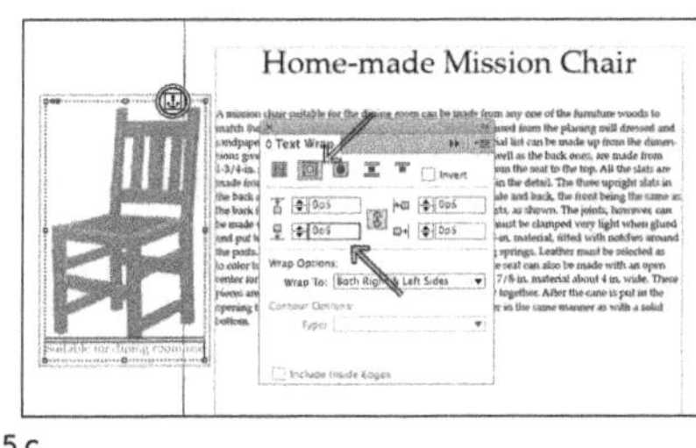


5 c

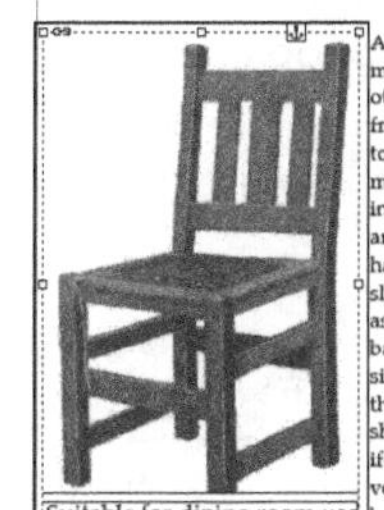


5 c

## Links and cross-references

One of the main advantages of ebooks over print is that they can contain links to additional information, whether in the same book or on an external website. InDesign makes it easy to incorporate links into your ebook. There are two main types of links: links which specify both the destination and the link text, and links in which the link text is automatically generated based on the text at the specified destination. This second type of link is called a cross-reference. It's a good idea to apply a character style to each type of link.

## Creating internal links within a book

1. First, determine the destination by selecting the location in the book where you want the link to point to, and choose New Hyperlink Destination from the panel menu of the Hyperlinks panel (accessed through Window > Interactive > Hyperlinks). Note the name of the Text Anchor, you'll need it later. By default, the name of the Text Anchor is the first few words of the destination text. Then click OK.
2. Next select the text that you want to convert into a link and choose New Hyperlink from the Hyperlinks panel menu.

3. Choose Text Anchor from the 'Link To' pull-down menu, then select the name of the document in which the destination Text Anchor can be found, and select the name of the Text Anchor.
4. It's also a good idea to apply a style so that you can format all the links later.
5. Click OK to create the link.

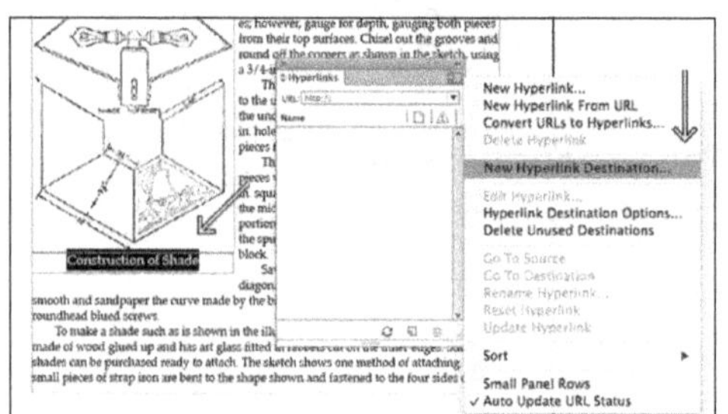


1

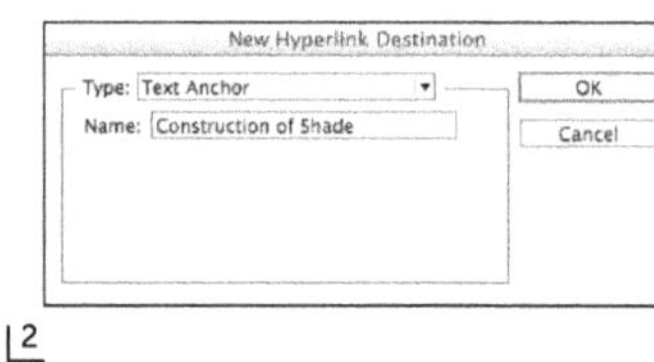


2

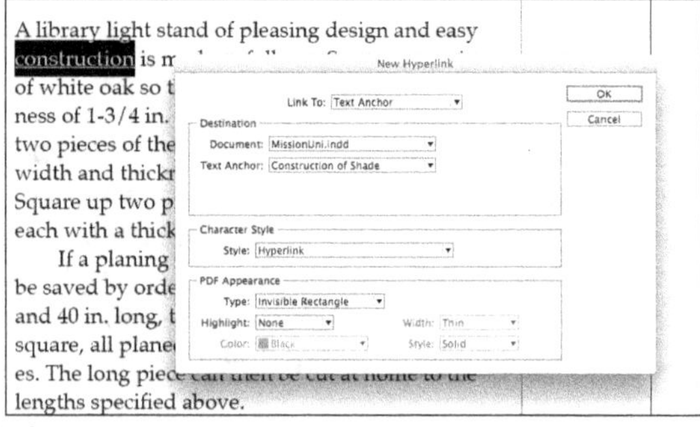


3 + 4

A library light stand of pleasin
construction is made as follow
of white oak so that it shall ha
ness of 1-3/4 in. with a length

5

## Creating cross-references

Cross-references are links in which the link text is automatically generated based on the text at the specified destination. A typical example of a cross-reference is a link to a different chapter or heading name. InDesign will always use the most up-to-date text in the heading.

1. To create a cross-reference, first place the cursor in the text where you want the link to appear.
2. To view the Cross-References panel, choose Window > Type & Tables > Cross-References.
3. Choose Insert Cross-Reference from the panel menu.
4. Under Destination, specify the desired Document. Then, from the list on the left-hand side, choose the type of paragraph you wish to link to. All paragraphs formatted with that particular style will show up in the list on the right-hand side, allowing you to choose the paragraph you want the cross-reference to link to.
5. Select a Cross-Reference Format, and click OK. The text from the destination will now appear in the body of your document. It will be exported as a link in the EPUB document.,

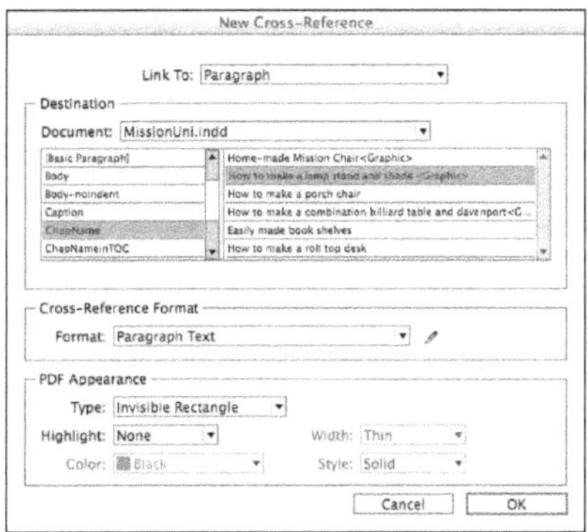


1 + 2 + 3 + 4

upholstered with leather in the same manner as with a solid bottom. Similar techniques are used in "How to make a lamp stand and shade"

5

## Tables of contents

Ebooks have two different types of tables of contents: the conventional one which is part of the text (more or less like any chapter in your book, only with links to the other chapters and sections); and one that is accessed through the menus of the user's e-reader device or application, regardless of which page the user is currently viewing.

InDesign facilitates the creation of both types. InDesign generates tables of contents based on styled paragraphs. For example, you might want to generate a table of contents based on all paragraphs formatted with the Heading 1 and Heading 2 styles, or as in the following example, based on all of the 'ChapName' elements.

### Creating a Table of Contents Style

1. Choose Layout > Table of Contents Styles and then click New in the dialog box that appears. The New Table of Contents Style dialog box will now appear.
2. Fill in the Title, for example 'Contents'. This will be used for the heading above the generated table of contents. Then choose which paragraph style to apply to that heading.
3. Choose which types of paragraph will be used to populate the table of contents, such as headings or chapter names.
4. Click More Options on the upper right-hand side of the dialog box (if this option is already selected, the option Fewer Options will appear instead).
5. In the area titled Style, choose which style to apply to each type of element in the table of contents. It's a good idea to create special styles for these elements.

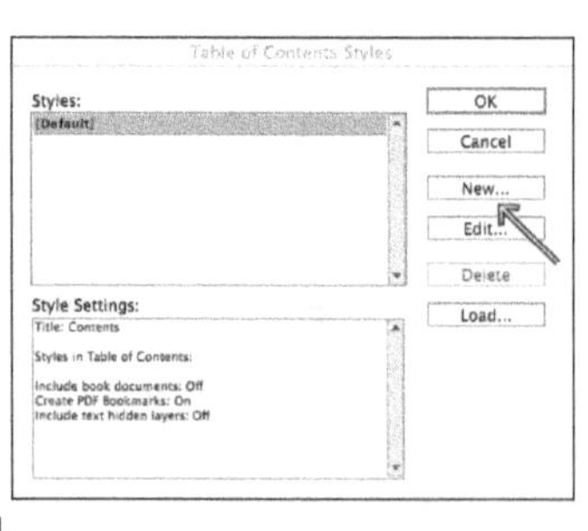


1

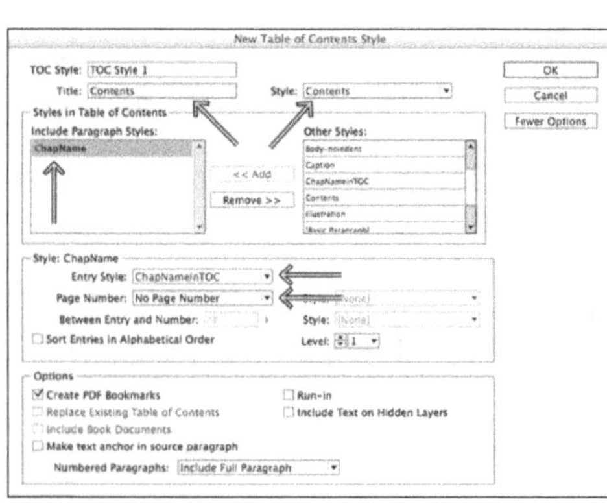


3 + 4 + 5 + 6 + 7

6. In the Page Number menu box, choose No Page Number, since page numbers are not necessary in an ebook.
7. Click OK to save the Table of Contents Style. This is the first step for creating both a navigational and an in-document table of contents.

**Generating the in-document table of contents**

1. Once you've created a Table of Contents Style, choose Layout > Table of Contents to have InDesign generate the table of contents by extracting the text from the paragraphs formatted in the styles you have selected.
2. Use the 'loaded' pointer to place the table of contents at the desired location in the document. You are not required to place the table of contents at the beginning of the book, or indeed to include it all.
3. You will learn how to generate the navigational table of contents in the Export Options section of this step-by-step guide.

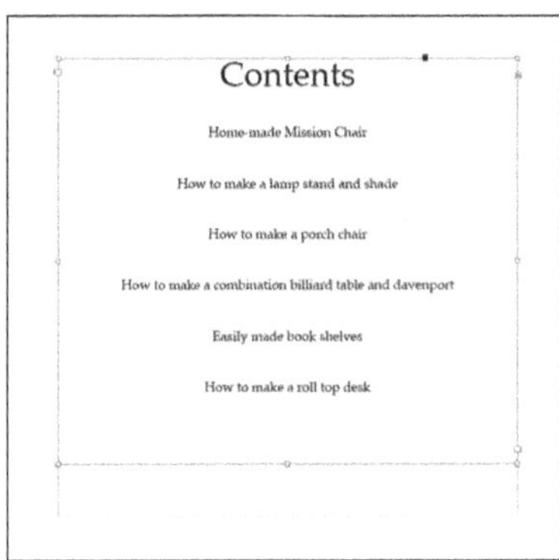


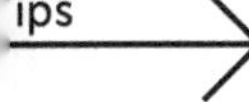

- **If you export a multi-document book to EPUB without having first created a Table of Contents Style, InDesign automatically creates a table of contents based on the filenames of the individual documents in the book. If you export a single-document book to EPUB, InDesign will not automatically generate a table of contents.**
- **You can create a navigational table of contents, an in-document table of contents, or both. Most e-readers will display an error message if no navigational table of contents is found. Some ebook stores will complain if you don't include an in-document table of contents.**

## Metadata

Metadata is information about your book, including the title of the publication, the name of the author, the names of other contributors, the publisher, date of publication, a description of the subject matter, keywords, copyright status, etc. It's a good idea to provide as much metadata as possible to make it easy for prospective readers to find your book.

InDesign gives you two opportunities to add metadata: in the File Info dialog box, and when you export your file to EPUB. The two sets of information overlap but are not identical. Empty fields will be filled in with data from the other set of information.

1. To add metadata to your file, go to File > File Info.
2. You can add additional metadata as you export the document to EPUB as discussed further below.

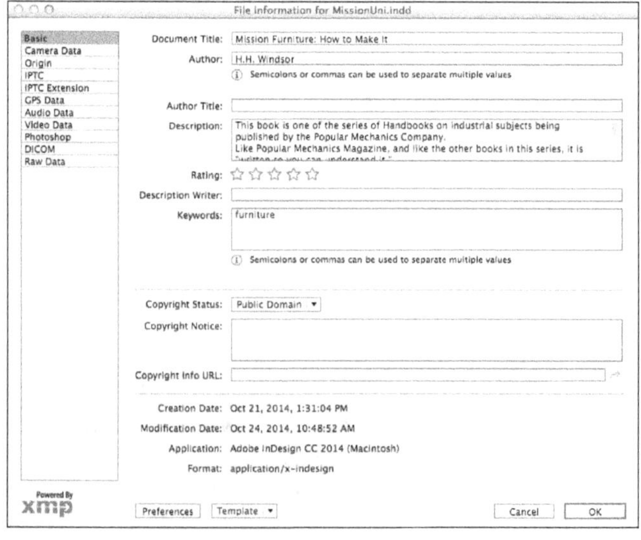

## Cover

The final step before exporting to EPUB is to create and add a cover image for your ebook. Because ebook covers are often viewed at small sizes, it's important to have large, clear text and to visually preview the cover at a very small ('icon') size. Of course the resolution of the image should also be high enough to look good at full-screen size as well. Most ebook stores require images that are at least 1000 pixels on the shortest side.

1. Create or edit the cover image (either in InDesign or in a graphics editor such as Photoshop) and save it in the JPEG format.
2. You will indicate the cover image to be used when you export to EPUB in the next section.

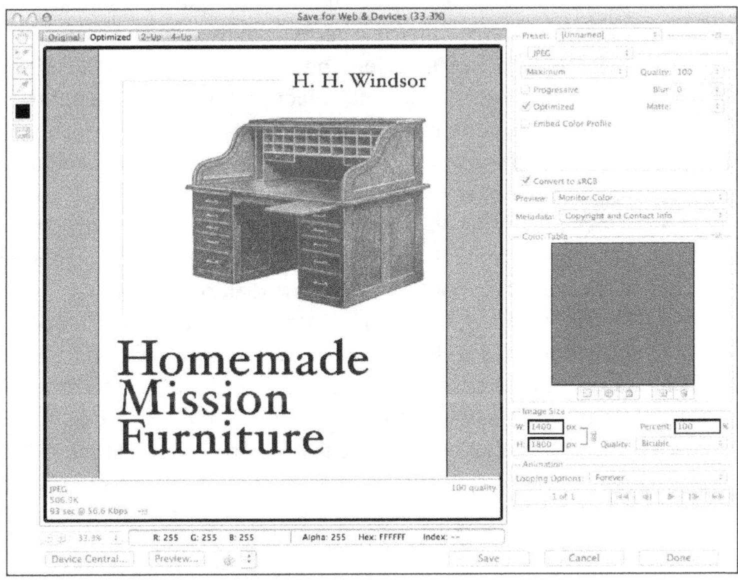

## Checklist and export options

Before finally exporting to EPUB, first make sure that all formatting has been applied using styles, that all images are properly placed and anchored, that you have defined all the necessary links and cross-references, that you have defined a Table of Contents Style, that you have specified all the necessary and desired metadata, and that you have created a high-resolution cover image that can also be viewed adequately at small sizes.

1. Select File > Export, then fill in a filename and destination, and select EPUB (Reflowable) from the Format pull-down menu.
2. Click Save. The 'EPUB – Reflowable Layout Export Options' dialog box appears with eight separate panels of options.
3. In the General panel, choose EPUB 3.0 from the Version pull-down-menu to ensure that your document complies with the latest standards.
4. Select the Choose Image option from the Cover pull-down menu; then navigate to the folder where you have saved the JPEG cover image you created earlier, and select that file. If you select the Rasterize Front Page option from the Cover pull-down menu instead, InDesign will create a snapshot of the first page of your book and use that image for the cover.
5. Select the option Multi Level (TOC Style) from the Navigation TOC pull-down menu; then choose the TOC Style that you created earlier in the New Table of Contents Style dialog box.
6. On the left-hand side of the dialog box, select the Metadata panel.
7. If the book has an ISBN, enter it in the Identifier field.
8. All the other fields besides the Date field should be automatically populated with data entered earlier in the File Info dialog box. You can add any missing information now. InDesign uses the information in the Date field for the EPUB2 element 'dc:date', but will use the actual date and time to automatically fill in this information in a format compatible with EPUB3. In other words, you don't have to enter anything in the Date field.
9. There are many other export options: for controlling how images and text are exported, for adding JavaScript and CSS, and for choosing how the ebook should be previewed. Feel free to explore these at your own leisure. The CSS panel has some of the most interesting options, since it allows you to override or even completely substitute the sometimes bulky and awkward CSS generated by InDesign with your own carefully crafted CSS.
10. Finally, click OK to generate the EPUB file.

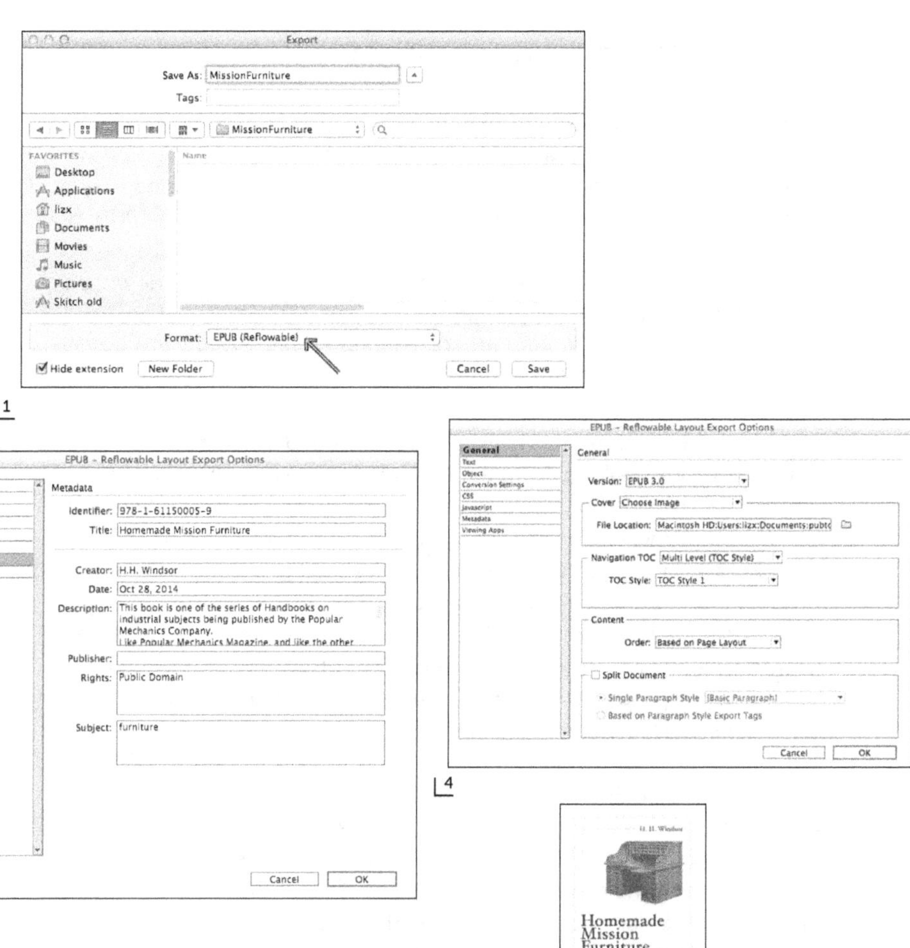


## Testing and validating

Be sure to test the EPUB file with as many e-reader devices and applications as possible. You can use the application Kindle Previewer to open the EPUB in a Kindle simulator and/or to convert the EPUB to the Kindle format so that you can test it on actual Kindle devices. Finally, it's always a good idea to validate your EPUB documents before releasing them.[7]

7 EPUB Validator (beta), http://validator.idpf.org.

## DO-IT-YOURSELF EPUB USING PANDOC

Pandoc and Calibre are two popular tools for converting documents to and from a wide variety of formats.[8] Both can be used to make EPUBs. First we will explore Pandoc; Calibre will be described in the next section. Using Pandoc, it is possible to convert even a Microsoft Word .docx file directly to EPUB; however this is not advisable. It is best to first convert the .docx file to a format which can be directly manipulated by the designer, such as Markdown which we will discuss more in detail in Chapter 7. ◺ (*Hybrid Workflow How-To: Making Automated Workflows, Part 1*) ◺ (*Hybrid Workflow How-To: Making Automated Workflows, Part 2*)

In this guide we will use the Old English epic poem *Beowulf* as a working example. The text is available from the Project Gutenberg website in a variety of formats (including EPUB). The 'plain text' version is the complete text of the poem in a single file with no styling whatsoever (no fonts, font sizes, formatting such as bold or italic, etc.). We will use this text to show how a simple conversion to EPUB can be done. Before starting, first download and install Pandoc.[9] Pandoc is a 'command-line' program, as opposed to a graphical user interface (GUI) environment, so once the software is installed you will not see a desktop icon with which to 'open' it. In the following step-by-step guide we will explain how to use the tool.

In order to make an EPUB of the *Beowulf* text using Pandoc, start by downloading the 'plain text' file from Project Gutenberg.[10] In your *Documents* folder, make a new subfolder and call it *pandoc-test*. This is the folder where we will be storing the documents to be converted, and retrieving the documents created by Pandoc. Save the file in this folder and name it *beowulf.txt*. To convert the file into an EPUB, follow the steps below.

1. First open *beowulf.txt* with Microsoft Word or a similar word processor. Save the file as a .docx document, named *beowulf.docx* and located in the same *pandoc-test* folder.

2. Pandoc is a command-line tool. To use it, you'll need to open a Terminal window (Mac) or Command Prompt window (Windows):

---

8 Pandoc: http://www.johnmacfarlane.net/pandoc/; Calibre ebook management: http://calibre-ebook.com/.

9 Installing pandoc, http://www.johnmacfarlane.net/pandoc/installing.html.

10 Beowulf by J. Lesslie Hall, http://www.gutenberg.org/ebooks/16328.

Mac: Open the Terminal from the *Utilities* subfolder in the *Applications* folder, or through the search bar at the top right of the screen. Note: Pandoc does not work on older Mac operating systems.

Windows: To open the Command Prompt window, first type Windows+R (hold down the Windows key and briefly press the R key) and then type 'cmd' and hit the enter key. You will see a new black-and-white window with a command prompt which should look something like 'C:\user\yourusername>'. <!-- \\ used to display \ in Markdown --> <!-- \> used to display > in Markdown -->

3. Whether in Mac or Windows, type 'cd documents' in order to 'change directory' (i.e. navigate) to the *Documents* folder.

4. Now type 'cd pandoc-test', again to change directory, this time to the subfolder within the *Documents* folder called *pandoc-test*. Now we can work with the documents in this folder.

5. To get a list of files in the current folder, on Mac type 'ls' (l as in lima, referring to 'list'), on Windows type 'dir'. The file *beowulf.docx* should be included in the list.

6. To convert the file from .docx to EPUB, type the following command line:

```
pandoc beowulf.docx -f docx -t epub -s -o beowulf.epub
```

The first term of the command line ('pandoc') indicates which program will process the command, in this case Pandoc. The second term tells Pandoc which file to process, in this case *beowulf.docx*. The following terms '-f docx -t epub' mean that the conversion will be from the .docx format to the EPUB format. The next term '-s' instructs Pandoc to create a 'standalone' file, with an appropriate header and footer, in other words a file which can be used immediately and doesn't need to be combined with other converted fragments. And the final term '-o beowulf.epub' tells Pandoc that the output file should be called *beowulf.epub*.

7. To check that the file was indeed created, type 'ls' or 'dir' again. You should now see the new file *beowulf.epub*.

8. Open the EPUB from the folder, or in the Terminal (Mac) type:

```
open beowulf.epub
```

9. Note that you can also start with Markdown as a source format (we will explore Markdown in detail in the following chapter). Open the text file in your Markdown editor and save it as a Markdown (.md) file. Type the following command in Pandoc to convert the Markdown file to EPUB:

```
pandoc beowulf.md -f markdown -t epub -s -o beowulf.epub
```

While developing this Toolkit we created an online graphical user interface which makes it possible to use Pandoc to convert .docx files to HTML, plain text, ICML (InDesign) and Markdown. This browser-based converter is freely accessible online.[11]

## USING CALIBRE AND CUSTOM PLUG-INS

Many other publishing tools are available, which roughly fall into two categories. One can be described as full-fledged editors, the other are tools which allow publishers to enhance existing publications with interactive features.

### Calibre

Calibre[12] has been described as a 'Swiss army knife' for reading, converting, authoring and cataloging ebooks. It is Open Source, runs on Windows, Mac OS X, and Linux (with identical graphical interfaces on all these platforms) and is being very actively developed, with frequent version updates. We recommend it, along with Pandoc, as a standard tool for all ebook publishers. There are also (older) alternatives such as Sigil[13] which was discontinued in

11 An overview can be found on the Digital Publishing Toolkit Software Showcase, http://pandoc.networkcultures.org/ or go directly to http://pandoc.networkcultures.org/hybrid.html.

12 Calibre, http://calibre-ebook.com/.

13 Sigil, The EPUB Editor, http://code.google.com/p/sigil.

February 2014, and the inexpensive commercial program Jutoh,[14] which also runs on Windows, Mac OS X and Linux. Jutoh provides an easy-to-use editor for ebooks, with a graphical user interface similar to that of Microsoft Word. However, it is less powerful as a document converter and ebook database. Calibre can be used to:

- Open and read EPUB files on a personal computer;
- Import documents in various ebook and electronic text formats (including .docx, RTF, HTML and plain text) and convert them to EPUB and other document formats including Amazon Kindle, PDF and RTF;
- Manage a local library/database of all imported ebooks, with easy editing of the bibliographical metadata of each ebook;
- Synchronize the user's ebook library with e-reader devices;
- Edit ebooks in HTML source code, with a live preview in a graphical user interface.

Calibre advertises itself as 'the one stop solution to all your ebook needs'. And indeed, (small) publishers can use Calibre as their single, one-size-fits-all tool for ebook production. Calibre is the most accessible and straightforward authoring software currently available for creating text-oriented, standards-compliant ebooks. However, Calibre's user interface can be confusing. The program has so many features and modules that it can feel like several programs jammed into one. When it comes to converting files, the graphical user interface of Calibre is perhaps more user-friendly, but Pandoc produces better results. Despite these limitations, Calibre is an excellent program for importing simple text documents, adjusting the formatting, and exporting the result to the most common ebook formats.

At the time of writing, the easiest and least expensive method of hybrid publishing is to convert the source text to Markdown, manually edit the Markdown into a well-structured document, use Pandoc to convert Markdown to EPUB, and import the EPUB into Calibre for final adjustments and conversion into other ebook formats (including Amazon Kindle).

14 Jutoh, epublishing made easy, http://www.jutoh.com.

## Enhancement utilities: Adobe Digital Publishing Suite, Mag+

These applications usually integrate (as custom plug-ins) with a previously installed Adobe InDesign package and allow designers to add interactive content (media, animations, etc.) to an ebook design. As such these tools are often used to convert print magazines into digital products suitable for sale on platforms such as Apple's Newsstand. Mag+ for example 'is based upon an InDesign plugin and made for creating tablet and smartphone apps without the need for programming skills'.[15]

## Other possibilities

For publications which require consistent design and uniform interactivity across devices, a reflowable document will probably not be the best solution. Therefore various publishers have developed their own (mobile) applications, such as The Guardian's iOS[16] version of its newspaper, the 'amplified' ebooks series by Penguin,[17] or the children's books published by Purple Carrot Books.[18] These solutions offer detailed control over interactivity as well as consistency of design, but at the extra cost of hiring a specialist (or even a team of specialists) to engineer the application. Transferring an EPUB to another device is fairly easy; however, publishing specifically for many platforms is by no means straightforward, due to the relatively closed nature of mobile operating systems. For example, an application designed specifically for the iPhone/iPad iOS Software Development Kit (SDK) will practically require a rewrite from scratch, even in a different programming language, before it can run on the Android platform.

Finally, why not simply publish essays, articles or even whole books on a website? The abundance of blogs and other publishing platforms shows that this is indeed a viable form of publishing. Monetizing is less straightforward: most

---

15 Mag + Mobile Publishing, https://www.magplus.com.

16 Guardian app for iOS and Android, http://www.theguardian.com/global/ng-interactive/2014/may/29/-sp-the-guardian-app-for-ios-and-android.

17 For example: Jack Kerouac's On the Road (A Penguin Books Amplified Edition), July 2, 2011, http://www.penguin.com/static/pages/features/amplified_editions/on_the_road.php</a> and Ayn Rand's Atlas Shrugged (An NAL Amplified Edition), October 12, 2013, http://www.penguin.com/static/pages/features/amplified_editions/atlas_shrugged.php.

18 The Prisoner of Carrot Castle, November 19, 2013, https://itunes.apple.com/us/app/the-prisoner-of-carrot-castle/id499981407?mt=8&ign-mpt=uo%3D4.

websites generate income by showing the user advertisements or sponsored articles. Paid membership is also a model used by some websites, such as the Dutch news platform *De Correspondent*.[19] One of the major downsides is that the content will only be available online, and cannot be easily transferred as a single unit of information the way an EPUB or PDF can.

19 De Correspondent, https://decorrespondent.nl.

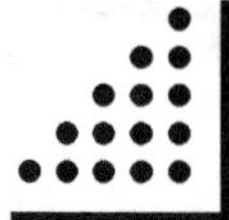

# 07

# TOWARDS A HYBRID WORKFLOW BASED ON MARKDOWN

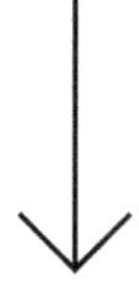

- Hybrid publishing gives the best results based on a single source document which can then be converted to different output formats (InDesign, EPUB, HTML, etc.).
- The traditional Microsoft Word + Adobe InDesign workflow does not work well for ebook publishing.
- Markdown, a plain-text format with simple markup, has many pragmatic advantages as a source format for hybrid publications.
- Markdown can be learned quickly, and makes clear formatting easy.
- There are many text editing and document conversion programs that support Markdown.
- XML is technically superior, but often too complex for small publishers.
- Hybrid publication projects can also be authored in database-driven content management systems, which have their own advantages and limitations.

## ELECTRONIC PUBLISHING WORKFLOWS: DESKTOP PUBLISHING AND MARKDOWN

Creating a workflow that is both structured and flexible enough to cater to a variety of demands is a key step towards establishing an efficient electronic or hybrid publishing strategy. What we propose here is a hybrid workflow based on the need for publishing across different media, while keeping the main part of the work process in-house rather than outsourcing it.

Instead of developing a digital publication based on the printed book at the end of a production process, as is common practice by publishers, the main workflow should be adapted at an earlier stage, and made efficient and practical for hybrid publishing. Development of each publication format from scratch is thus superseded by single-source, multi-format publishing. In other words: rather than working separately on the PDF for the print book, the EPUB version, and a Kindle edition, the workflow is instead focused on a single source file (in the Markdown format) which can easily be converted into these different output formats using a relatively small number of digital tools.

The workflow described below starts at the point when the author hands in the final manuscript, in other words after the editing and rewriting process has been completed. In reality this is of course not the beginning of the publishing process. However, rewriting and editing is still most efficiently done using word processing applications with full tracking and commenting functions, such as Microsoft Word. Also, in our experience manuscripts are mainly written in Word and delivered in .doc or .docx files. Should the author already be working or submitting manuscripts in the Markdown, HTML or even XML format, this will of course affect the workflow.

Note: an important step preceding the publication process lies in the formulation of an in-house style guide in which authors and editors can find the requirements for the manuscript. This style guide must be adapted according to the hybrid workflow before starting any work on the manuscript itself. For example: specification of the required file format, structuring of the text, image specifications, etc. See Chapter 8 for more information on adapting the style guide. ◺ (*Style Guide for Hybrid Publishing*)

We will now focus on the implementation of the new workflow for small-edition and low-budget publishing houses. ◺ (*Hybrid workflow how-to: introduction & editorial steps*)

# TRADITIONAL WORKFLOW

text
IMPORT
.indd
STRUCTURE
.indd
SOURCE

DESIGN
DESIGN
COPY

.indd
EXPORT
.indd
EXPORT
text
STRUCTURE

EPUB
DEVELOP
PDF
PRINT
HTML
DEVELOP
DESIGN

## Desktop publishing workflow (from Word to InDesign to electronic book)

A brief description of the desktop publishing (DTP) workflow currently used by many publishers would be: a Microsoft Word file is imported into InDesign and, after designing and editing, exported to PDF, ready to be printed. After work on the printed edition has been completed, the book may be converted into an electronic version which follows the design of the 'original' as closely as possible. This traditional, print-oriented workflow can be seen as the standard for one-to-one publications.

There are certain advantages to this workflow: it is simple and linear, and there are no version branches. You end up with one consolidated manuscript, and What You See Is What You Get (WYSIWYG) when it comes to design. For example, in the case of a fixed-layout print design, adjustments in the hyphenation may need to be done manually in the InDesign document. In digital publishing however, hyphenations are never fixed, but are subject to change as the layout is reflowed according to the requirements of the device used. Therefore, if an editorial correction involves a change in hyphenation, this need not (or cannot) be adjusted in the digital file. This saves some work, but also means a limitation in the possibilities for electronic design.

The main disadvantage of the DTP workflow in 'going electronic' is that it is focused on one single medium, and that the steps to go from there to a digital edition are quite laborious and do not make full use of the possibilities offered by electronic publishing. It is relatively straightforward to generate an EPUB based on the InDesign file, however in order to make use of the full possibilities offered by hybrid publishing (such as modular publishing, immediate updating, optimal uses of audio and visual formats), one should take these possibilities into consideration from the very beginning. A workflow that is based on print publishing generally attempts to convert the paper book into an electronic book at the last stage of the process.

Converting an InDesign document to an electronic publication is not an ideal solution, especially when working with older versions of the software. The InDesign file in this case is automatically converted to HTML code which can be messy, sometimes even too messy to be rendered properly on an e-reader device or application. ◺ (*Notes on EPUB Development in Adobe InDesign CS6*) The results of the conversion may require additional steps in order to finalize the publication.[1] The most recent version of InDesign (InDesign CC) has improved functionality for electronic publishing, but requires very careful structuring and preparation of documents in order to yield good results within reasonable work times. It is best suited for projects in which the content is generated from databases, imported as XML into InDesign and from there exported to EPUB. For a detailed look at these developments, see also the step-by-step guide describing how to convert a document from InDesign to EPUB. It is possible to create 'interactive' publications in the PDF format, working with Microsoft Word and InDesign. In the end however these are also static InDesign documents, upgraded with some interactive layers. This is still a limited vision of the possibilities of digital publishing.

## From Microsoft Word (.docx) to EPUB

Desktop publishing applications such as InDesign, and WYSIWYG word processors such as Microsoft Word or OpenOffice, are generally not well suited for processing structured text (see Chapter 2, The basics). Though it is possible to work in a structured manner, for example by using style definitions rather than manually applying formatting, the user is not required to make a distinction between formatting and structure, which is essential in the world of digital publishing.

There is a viable solution for generating an EPUB from a Microsoft Word .docx file using the latest version of the command-line tool Pandoc, a powerful universal document converter.[2] However, since Word does not, as explained above, enforce good structure in a document, the EPUB generated by Pandoc will always be imperfect and thus not ready for publishing. Still, it should provide a relatively clean foundation for a designer to produce the final ebook. Other Word-to-EPUB programs, such as the built-in document converter of Calibre, (*Converting a Docx directly to EPUB using Calibre*) produce less satisfying results.

In order to obtain the best possible EPUB file, the .docx file should be formatted using only Word's standard paragraph styles such as 'Normal', 'Title', 'Subtitle', 'Quote' and most importantly 'Heading 1', 'Heading 2', 'Heading 3' for

1 Elizabeth Castro has provided a thorough guide for InDesign-to-EPUB publication in her book EPUB Straight to the Point, San Francisco: Peachpit Press, 2010.

2 Pandoc a universal document converter, http://www.johnmacfarlane.net/pandoc/.

the headings according to their logical hierarchy. For example: 'Heading 1' for chapters, 'Heading 2' for sections, 'Heading 3' for sub-sections. Since the resulting EPUB document will contain a table of contents and document navigation menu based on the 'Heading' hierarchy, a proper structuring of headings is crucial. Word footnotes will appear as linked endnotes in the EPUB, thereby elegantly simplifying an otherwise tedious document redesign task.

Word unfortunately lacks two features that would make it more suitable for hybrid publishing projects:

1. Word does not have a 'strict mode' that would 'force' all writers and editors of a document to use only defined paragraph styles instead of manual formatting. This means that your document will likely contain headings that haven't been defined as headings, but are just bold-faced text, quotes that haven't been defined as quotes, etc. Unfortunately, if the manual formatting has the same visual appearance as the predefined paragraph styles, it can be hard or even impossible to locate all instances in the document.
2. Word provides no automatic or semi-automatic tools for finding manual formatting and replacing it with predefined paragraph styles. The only way to achieve this is to manually review and adjust the whole document.

Often, such inconsistencies in a Word document will only become visible after the EPUB conversion, for example as a missing chapter heading in the table of contents of the ebook. These are the inherent risks and limitations of using Word in the editorial workflow. Nevertheless, the Word-plus-Pandoc option will likely be the easiest and least painful solution for publishers.

We recommend two ways of working with Word + Pandoc.

1. Conversion from Word to EPUB using Pandoc directly from the Terminal (Mac) / Command Prompt (Windows), or using the browser-based converter developed for this Toolkit.[3] This should only be done only at the very end of the editorial process, because after this conversion no further editorial changes can be applied to the Word

3 An overview can be found on the Digital Publishing Toolkit Software Showcase, http://pandoc.networkcultures.org/ or go directly to http://pandoc.networkcultures.org/hybrid.html.

document. A graphic designer can quite easily transform the converted document into the final electronic publication (for example, by modifying the typographic design to make it suitable for e-readers, by scaling and optimizing images for screen reading, by adding bibliographical metadata, etc.).

2. Conversion from Word to Markdown using Pandoc. Since Pandoc can also convert files *to* the Markdown format, this is often the preferable option, especially for complex publishing projects. The resulting Markdown file can then be used as the 'master file' for conversions to various other file formats (such as EPUB, or HTML for publishing on a website). The advantage of converting to Markdown is that any formatting glitch in the Word document will now become clearly visible. For example, a heading formatted manually will be converted as **heading** while a heading formatted with the proper style definition will be converted as #heading. This makes it much easier to clean up the internal formatting of the document and produce a 'clean' master file for all subsequent document conversions. The EPUB generated from this Markdown file will in most cases be much better structured than an EPUB directly generated from the Word file, making the subsequent work to be performed by the designer much easier. It is also possible to customize the Pandoc conversion by defining style templates. This in turn may make it possible, depending on the type and complexity of the publication, to automatically generate a complete and well-formatted EPUB from the Markdown files without even having to hire a designer.

We would advise against using Pandoc to convert back and forth between Word and EPUB. If the Word document is subject to further editorial changes, then the conversion to EPUB (as in the first scenario) should be done again, as would any work already done by the designer on the previously exported EPUB file. Therefore, if possible the editorial changes should be implemented directly in the EPUB or Markdown file.

# MARKDOWN WORKFLOW

.md
SOURCE
CONVERT
.icml
IMPORT DESIGN
.indd
EXPORT
PDF
PRINT
EPUB
CONVERT
DEVELOP DESIGN

## Cleaning up Markdown

Since Markdown is not a word processing application but a document format, it does not provide functions such as automatic renumbering of footnotes and list items. In fact, such numbers don't matter since everything will be renumbered during the document conversion anyway.

However, Pandoc can be used to 'clean up' the Markdown source text; the trick is to convert the document *from* Markdown *to* Markdown. Open a Terminal window (Mac) or Command Prompt window (Windows) and type the following line (be sure to first place the file in the appropriate folder and to navigate to that folder, as explained in detail in Chapter 6.

```
pandoc beowulf.md -f markdown -t markdown -o beowulf_clean.md
```

This means that the program Pandoc is instructed to convert the file *beowulf.md* file from markdown ('-f markdown') to markdown ('-t markdown') and save the (cleaned up) result in a new file called led *beowulf_clean.md* ('-o beowulf_clean.md').

## Markdown workflow

As mentioned above, we recommend the use of the markup language Markdown as part of a hybrid workflow. Though Markdown is not perfect, it is much easier to work with than, say, the complex markup language XML. Markdown allows for the creation of structured texts, an important requirement in hybrid publishing. ◺ (*Mark me up, mark me down*)

**Introduction: advantages and limitations**
John Gruber, the creator and main developer of Markdown, describes Markdown on his website as follows: 'Markdown allows you to write using an easy-to-read, easy-to-write plain-text format, then convert it to structurally valid XHTML (or HTML).'[4] In other words, Markdown is a way of formatting plain text using human-readable formatting symbols, rather than HTML-style tags such as <b> for bold or <h1> to define a top-level heading. For example, this is what the beginning of *Alice's Adventures in Wonderland* would like in Markdown:

4 John Gruber, Markdown: Introduction, daringfireball.net/projects/markdown/.

```
#Alice's Adventures in Wonderland
##Chapter I. Down the Rabbit-Hole

There was nothing so _very_ remarkable in that; nor
did Alice think it so VERY much out of the way to
hear the Rabbit say to itself,

> Oh dear! Oh dear!
> I shall be late!

(when she thought it over afterwards, it occurred to
her that she ought to have wondered at this, but at
the time it all seemed quite natural); but when the
Rabbit actually **took a watch out of its waistcoat-
pocket**, and looked at it, and then hurried on,
Alice started to her feet, for it flashed across her
mind that she had never before seen a rabbit with
either a waistcoat-pocket, or a watch to take out of
it, and burning with curiosity, she ran across
the field after it, and fortunately was just in time
to see it pop down a large rabbit-hole under the
hedge.
```

**Alice's Adventures in Wonderland**

**Chapter I. Down the Rabbit-Hole**

There was nothing so *very* remarkable in that; nor did Alice think it so VERY much out of the way to hear the Rabbit say to itself,

> *Oh dear! Oh dear! I shall be late!*

(when she thought it over afterwards, it occurred to her that she ought to have wondered at this, but at the time it all seemed quite natural); but when the Rabbit actually **took a watch out of its waistcoat-pocket**, and looked at it, and then hurried on, Alice started to her feet, for it flashed across her mind that she had never before seen a rabbit with either a waistcoat-pocket, or a watch to take out of it, and burning with curiosity, she ran across the field after it, and fortunately was just in time to see it pop down a large rabbit-hole under the hedge.

In this example, the tag '#' defines a top-level heading, '##' a second-level heading, '_' italic text, '**' bold text, and '>' a block quote. Markdown also provides tags for defining lists, embedded images, and links. The popular extended version MultiMarkdown provides further support for footnotes, tables, mathematical formulas, cross-references, bibliographies and definition lists. Using simple Open Source conversion applications such as Pandoc, text formatted using Markdown can be automatically converted to well-structured HTML, EPUB, PDF, RTF or other document formats, requiring no manual adjustments.

Markdown is a product of internet culture. It uses ad-hoc formatting signs commonly used in e-mail and chat platforms, and further popularized on blogging platforms, to provide a standardized, human-readable, user-friendly and well-structured document format, suitable for long-term storage and as a basic source for conversions to contemporary and future document formats. While its formatting syntax is simple, it is also both strict and unambiguous enough to allow multiple writers and editors to work on a single document without unnecessary confusion. Another advantage of Markdown is that it can be written and edited in any software application capable of processing basic text: unlike the proprietary file formats of Microsoft Word or other word processors, Markdown can be opened using a simple text editor.

Why do we recommend Markdown in particular? For certain publishing projects – for example, handbooks or books derived from wikis, it may be worth considering alternatives to Markdown, such as *reStructuredText*. There are, however, two reasons why we recommend Markdown as a practical tool for electronic and mixed-media publishing:

1. Excellent software support. There are many user-friendly, high quality applications for writing and editing documents in Markdown and for converting Markdown to other formats. While Markdown may be written and edited in any text editor, there are several user-friendly text editing applications that make it easier to edit and immediately view the results, such as Mou, MacDown, Texts, MarkdownPad, UberWriter and MdCharm.
2. The extended version MultiMarkdown provides all the necessary formatting and document syntax needed for text-oriented publishing in the arts and humanities, or the text component (complete with footnotes and bibliographical references) of an exhibition catalog.

However, Markdown/MultiMarkdown is not a magical one-size-fits-all solution. It is particularly well suited for text-oriented documents, but quite limited for creating visually oriented documents, and not really of much use for interactive publishing formats. Markdown and similar formatting/markup languages are designed for workflows in which there is a clear separation between editorial work (involving writers, translators and editors) and publication design. For publications requiring extensive interaction between writers/editors and visual designers/artists from the very beginning of the authoring process, other tools and workflows are preferable.

**Markdown vs. XML**

XML is designed for creating structured documents with a clear separation between logical structure and visual formatting. It is the most detailed structuring and formatting language ever developed, and provides the foundation for many other such languages. For example, both HTML and Microsoft Word's .docx are XML-based document formats. So why shouldn't we use XML then? While XML theoretically provides an ideal way of working with single-format files to produce multiple output formats, we do not recommend it for small, independent publishing houses.

The main reason for this is that the broad versatility of XML adds several layers of complexity. Markdown on the other hand can easily be used by non-technical users while still providing good structure and better document conversion into HTML, EPUB and many other formats than Microsoft Word and similar word processing applications.

Technically speaking, Markdown provides some of the same features and advantages as XML does, namely separation of content structure from visual layout and painless conversion into multiple output formats. However, unlike XML, it cannot be extended with custom, self-defined markup tags. Still, and particularly for those just getting started with digital or hybrid publishing, Markdown should be more than adequate in almost all circumstances.

Word processing / editing applications for Markdown

**Mac**

*Freeware:*

- Mou[5], with features such as live preview, sync scroll, auto save, auto pair, custom themes, CSS, HTML and PDF export, enhanced CJK support, and more.
- MacDown[6], released under the MIT License and with a design and setup influenced by Mou.

*Paid:*

- Byword[7], a user-friendly, distraction-free text writing program with built-in MultiMarkdown support and export to HTML, RTF, PDF and Microsoft Word. The program runs on Mac, iPhone and iPad.
- A Writer[8], a program similar to Byword. The program runs on Mac, iPhone and iPad.
- Scrivener[9], a word processing application popular among professional writers, available for Mac OS X and Windows. Fully supports MultiMarkdown internally.

**Windows**

- MarkdownPad[10], free for personal use; a paid upgrade to Markdown-Pad Pro unlocks additional features.

**Linux**

- UberWriter[11], this editor also includes built-in support for Pandoc.
- MdCharm[12], supports MultiMarkdown.

---

5 Mou, http://25.io/mou/.

6 MacDown, The Open Source Markdown editor for OS X, http://macdown.uranusjr.com/.

7 Byword 2, http://bywordapp.com/.

8 iA Writer, http://www.iawriter.com/mac/.

9 Scrivener 2, http://www.literatureandlatte.com/scrivener.php.

10 MarkdownPad, http://markdownpad.com/.

11 UberWriter, http://uberwriter.wolfvollprecht.de/.

12 MdCharm, http://www.mdcharm.com/.

**Document conversion programs**

- MultiMarkdown[13]: the original application converts MultiMarkdown files into HTML, PDF, and OpenDocument (for later conversion to RTF or Microsoft Word). Open Source, runs on Linux, Mac OS X and Windows.
- Pandoc[14]: similar in functionality to MultiMarkdown, but much more powerful. Pandoc reads more input formats (including HTML and reStructuredText) and can output HTML5, XHTML, LaTeX, RTF, Word, EPUB2 and EPUB3, PDF and many more. Typographical templates for the conversion can be easily customized ⊾ *(Docx to Markdown using Calibre and Pandoc)*.
- Calibre[15]: an Open Source application which allows users to manage ebook collections and to create, edit, and view ebooks. It supports a variety of formats (including the common Amazon Kindle and EPUB formats), ebook syncing with a variety of ebook readers, and conversion (within DRM restrictions) from various ebook and non-ebook formats. It runs on Linux, Mac OS X and Windows.

We recommend working with Pandoc in combination with Markdown. Both tools were used extensively in creating this publication.

**A note on limitations**

A major downside of Markdown is that it exists in several variants, each with its own extensions of the basic Markdown syntax. In the context of this Toolkit, we recommend the widespread variant MultiMarkdown which includes syntax for footnotes, tables, citations, cross-references, image captions and document metadata. It is also fully supported by Pandoc.

Another downside is that Markdown allows some formatting to be marked in alternative ways (for example, _underlines_ or *asterisks* both produce italic text) which can introduce inconsistency in a collaboratively edited document. However, as mentioned earlier, Pandoc can be used for eliminating such inconsistencies by converting from Markdown to Markdown.

At the time of writing, in late 2014, a standardization effort of Markdown and its extensions is underway, under the name 'CommonMark'.[16]

---

13 MultiMarkdown, http://fletcherpenney.net/multimarkdown/.

14 Pandoc, http://johnmacfarlane.net/pandoc/.

15 Calibre ebook management, http://calibre-ebook.com/.

16 Jeff Atwood, 'Standard Markdown is now Common Markdown', Coding Horror, http://blog.codinghorror.com/standard-markdown-is-now-common-markdown/.

## DATABASE PUBLISHING

What are the advantages of shifting to a hybrid publishing workflow? First of all, it will make much more efficient the process of creating a publication with multiple output formats. But this is only the beginning: when the hybrid workflow is comprehensively applied, when you really 'change your life', many new possibilities will open up. The most important of these, database publishing using a content management system, will be briefly discussed here.

A database is a collection of independent, yet mutually related, objects. These objects can be everything from structured texts to images of eighteenth-century paintings. An important point here is that we need clear structures that go beyond the short-term use of the database. Consider for example a company mailing list. We may take a person's full name and address as a single object. But if we wish to select by postal code or any other subcategory within the full name and address, or if we want to add more information to the person's name, such as age, e-mail address and previous purchases, we have to define a more detailed structure of objects and sub-objects, including their interdependencies (for example, a house number requires a street name and vice versa), whether or not they are mandatory (age may be optional), and so on. This makes building and maintaining the all-encompassing database difficult and time-consuming.

The best option is therefore to explicitly define the goals of the publication program as well as any practical limitations. The four publishing genres discussed in this publication all have their own requirements regarding the creation and distribution of publications. An art catalog requires clear descriptors for the identity of the artist, the materials used, the sizes, the image source, copyright, keywords according to established lists, etc. Other collections of images may require other data.

In pure text databases we also have to be careful. On one hand we have the data related to the author's name, affiliation, address, etc. But it becomes a different proposition when illustrations and diagrams are included and perhaps even shared between publications. If this is the case, we might consider a special section in our database that pertains only to illustrations and their descriptions. The same is true for bibliographical references and the collection of hyperlinks used in the text. Therefore we would advise that various objects such as image or text entities are provided with as many consistent metadata (field descriptors) as possible.

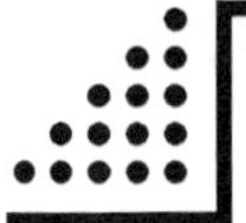

# 08

# GUIDE: HYBRID PUBLISHING FOR EACH GENRE

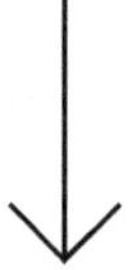

- Enforcing clearly defined style guides for all contributors can help simplify the process of hybrid publishing.
- Research publications can be converted or adapted to electronic publishing in a relatively straightforward manner with document conversion software.
- Exhibition catalogues can best be broken up into micro-publications, thus making them more suitable for reading on electronic devices. If this is not an option, then PDF is usually a more better format than EPUB for such publications.
- There is no 'standard recipe' for electronic artists' and designers' books. These books can be published in a wide variety of formats, even as plain-text files or animated GIFs. More conventional scenarios include publishing artists' blogs as ebooks.
- PDF files and WordPress blogs are currently the two most common electronic publication formats for art and design periodicals. With the emergence of HTML5 and new distribution platforms, this genre is in a state of ongoing transition.

## GENERAL CONSIDERATIONS

Following the step-by-step guide to making a simple EPUB (Chapter 6) and the general introduction to workflows for hybrid publishing (Chapter 7), we will now address a number of considerations that are specific to each of the most common publication genres in the field of arts and culture, as described in chapter 3.

The following points, which apply to all genres, should be clearly defined at the beginning of any hybrid publication project:

- Will the publication be medium-specific or medium-neutral? In other words, is the project a one-to-one conversion of a print book into an electronic book, or will the project include content and design elements that can only be realized with electronic media? One should also consider that many of the advantages of a hybrid publishing approach, as pointed out earlier, lie in modularized or database publishing. By dividing a larger work into small modules or 'building blocks', it is easier to generate custom publications, to apply updates to some parts only, to replace 'heavy' high-resolution images or other media files with 'lighter' ones when necessary, etc.
- Metadata is significantly more important in the context of hybrid publishing than it is in traditional print publishing. Carefully applied metadata will ensure that the publication can be found online in databases and bookstores such as Amazon, and will also make the electronic editing and design process more efficient. Especially in the case of modularized or database publishing, it is of utmost importance to start gathering metadata as early as possible in the production process. Otherwise it soon becomes impossible to meaningfully keep track of, and put together, the modular building blocks of the source document.
- For publishers in the field of arts and culture, file sizes pose a fundamental problem: on one hand, electronic publication seems to offer new opportunities for including multimedia and other possibilities not provided by 'static' print publishing; on the other hand, in the real world this often results in files that will be too large to be downloaded, stored or 'flipped through' in a practical manner.

When it comes to choosing a publication format, the following general recommendations should be kept in mind:

- EPUB is a good choice for ebooks, less so for periodicals. EPUB potentially combines the advantages of PDF (single-file distribution) with HTML (reflowable/screen size-independent design, small file sizes, modularity/reusability, automation).
- At the time of writing, HTML5 is theoretically the 'ideal' format. It is increasingly used in multimedia journalism (a good example is the report 'Snow Fall' published in *The New York Times* in December 2012 ). However this poses three important problems for publishers: the format is not supported by ebook stores such as iBooks and Kobo; it lacks the rich metadata support of EPUB; and it requires technical workarounds in order to allow for single-file distribution.
- PDF is the easiest format to integrate in existing workflows, but since it is essentially meant for print, it too has disadvantages when it comes to electronic publishing. It is a fixed-layout format, meaning that it does not dynamically reflow to adapt to different screen dimensions; it provides only rudimentary multimedia support; and the files can quickly become too large for the purposes intended.

## RESEARCH PUBLICATION

In pragmatic terms, electronic research publishing in the near future will focus on converting print versions of conventionally designed papers, journals and textbooks into digital editions. The fact that research publications tend to have highly structured formatting and are mainly text-based makes them ideal candidates for modularization and database publishing. This can lead to new possibilities in which the electronic publication takes on new forms which are not possible in the print edition.

### Workflows

In print research publications, the typical workflow is as follows:

- An editor works with the author(s) on the manuscript.
- Several versions of the manuscript are passed back and forth be-

tween several people in different roles (editor, author, copy editor, designer).
- The final version of the manuscript is established in a word processor (typically Microsoft Word) or a desktop publishing program (typically Adobe InDesign).
- A graphic designer designs the publication in InDesign.
- Corrections are made to the print proof and implemented in the InDesign file.
- A PDF file of the corrected InDesign file is sent to the printer. In Chapter 6 we described how to generate an electronic book based on an InDesign project. This requires a meticulous internal structuring of the InDesign document, something that is untypical for the typical workflow in book projects, and for which most graphic designers working with InDesign have not been trained. There is also another way to make use of the possibilities offered by hybrid publishing: rather than designing for print and then adding the electronic book as an afterthought at the end of the process, the publishing process is instead geared towards multiple output formats from the start.

This new workflow allows for a hybrid output to various media (including print, ebook and web) and is centered on a single editorial and archival file format, a finalized version of the source document from which multiple outputs can be generated. Instead of a Word document which is further modified in InDesign – both of which are less than optimal formats for converting to EPUB – the editorial and archival file will instead be in a format that can easily be converted to InDesign for the print edition and to EPUB, MOBI or web for the electronic publication. As explained earlier in chapters 6 and 7, the most suitable format for this workflow is Markdown, augmented with the additional MultiMarkdown extension (which allows for footnotes, cross-references and bibliographies), and subsequent conversion to InDesign, EPUB and web, which is then a very straightforward procedure using the Open Source software tool Pandoc.

# RESEARCH PUBLICATION

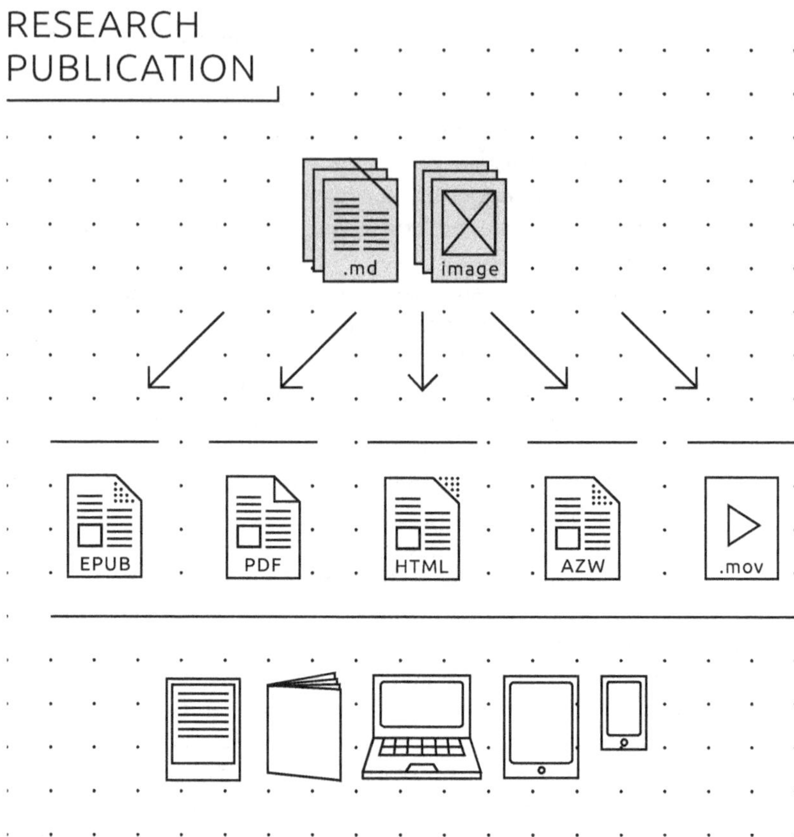


A hybrid workflow, focused on print as well as electronic publications, offers a number of advantages:

- Easy conversion into various electronic file formats.
- The possibility of collaborative editing and revision control, using resources ranging from simple user-friendly tools such as wikis and blogs to sophisticated revision control systems such as Git and GitHub (originally used for software development by teams of programmers working internationally on large projects).
- The possibility of adding elements other than text (videos, images, links) while keeping these separate from the main document files. This way, the size of the central editorial document remains very small, while images and videos in various resolutions for various

publication media are easier to maintain.

- Easy extraction of output derived from the book itself, such as abstracts, video book trailers, newsletters, or personalized electronic publications.
- Easier extraction of parts of a publication which can then be published separately.
- Independence from any particular software program (such as Word and InDesign).
- Long-term archivability.

## Style guide

A new workflow will require taking a number of measures in order to ensure suitable source documents for publication. First of all, it is necessary to communicate the details of the workflow to all contributors (authors, editors, designers) involved in the publishing process. Publication style guides must be adjusted accordingly and must specify:

- The file format to be submitted by contributors (for example: Markdown or .docx).
- If the file format is .docx, contributors should be required to use predefined paragraph and character styles for all formatting (such as 'Heading 1', 'Heading 2', 'Quote', etc.), and to absolutely avoid any direct text formatting other than italic or bold. Microsoft provides a useful introduction on this subject.
- Image style and format: only high-resolution images that are suitable for print but can also be downsized to lower resolutions for electronic publication.
- Metadata to be provided by the contributors such as keywords, contact information, abstract, biography.

There may also be different editorial criteria for the content in a hybrid workflow:

- Different style of writing: 'writing for the web' vs. 'writing for print'.
- The inclusion of interactive material, audio and video, as well as additional or other images for print.
- Metadata to be added by the editor/publisher. ⦣ (*Style Guide for Hybrid Publishing*)

# CATALOGUE PUBLICATION

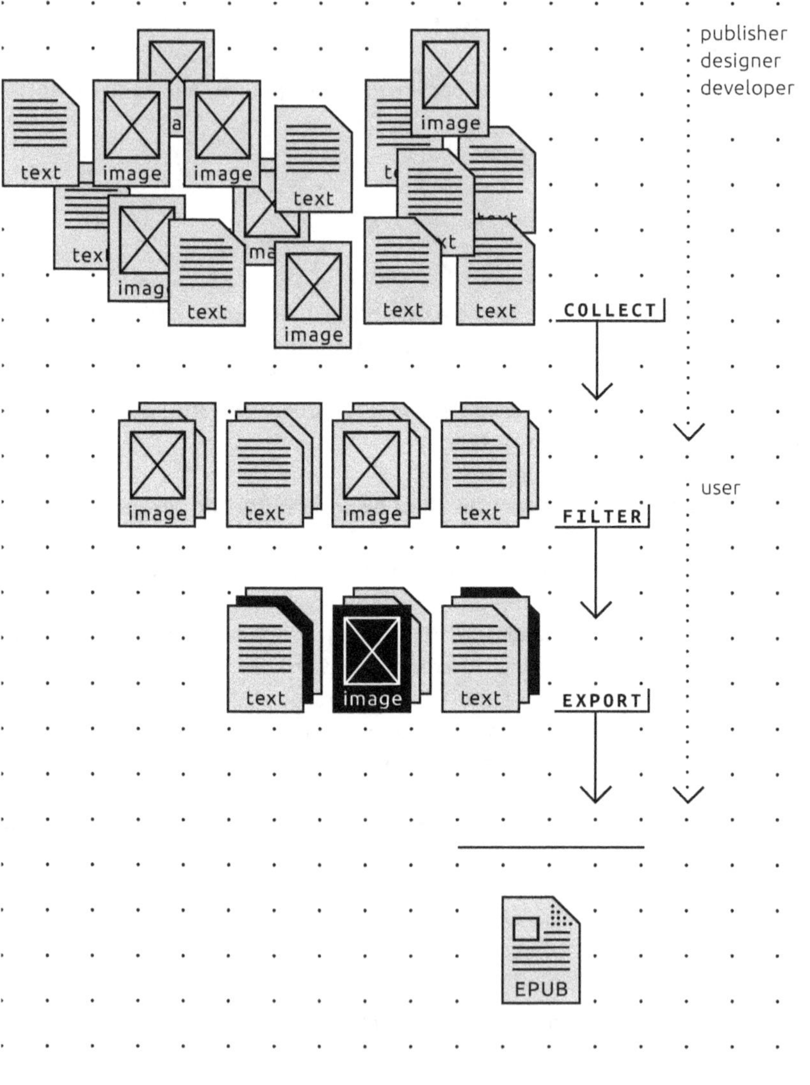

## ART/DESIGN CATALOGUE

The traditional workflow for an art/design catalogue is roughly the same as the InDesign workflow described for research publications, and focused on the production of one 'unified' book. The 'new' workflow however is based on a highly modularized publication process. The catalogue is built up of multiple modules or building blocks, for example different paintings, each with its own description, all following a standardized format. By considering these modules as separate entities and by storing, describing and tagging them as such, it becomes possible to generate customized publications using specific selections of the building blocks.

This also provides a solution for the problem of the publication's file size. In most cases, due to current limitations in bandwidth and storage space, an art catalogue is difficult to convert one-to-one to an electronic publication which can be downloaded within a reasonable amount of time. Therefore it is advisable to split up the publication into smaller sub-publications, such as monographic micro-ebooks on single art works, or collections of articles from which each reader can individually choose, thereby automatically generating a customized ebook. Modularized content can also lead to different commercial strategies, for example by offering parts of a publication through an 'in-app' download. An example of this is a project by the Stedelijk Museum in Amsterdam, which resulted in the MyHighlights app.

On a more philosophical level, we may well wonder whether a catalogue in the traditional sense actually constitutes a desirable publication genre for electronic publishing. It is of course interesting and exciting to consider new forms of small and smart catalogues, such as the micro-ebooks mentioned above. However, we will have to wait for increased storage capacity on portable devices, as well as faster mobile network speeds, before we can start to enjoy the full potential of these new forms. Currently, producing a high-resolution electronic catalogue of 100 pages or more only really makes sense as a large PDF file designed for desktop computer viewing.

### Workflows

In the specific case of art and design catalogues, the following changes to the workflow should be taken into consideration:

- Modularize the content and offer multiple small portions of a catalogue, i.e. one art work for each entry, separate images, videos, texts, etc.
- Make sure that each module is tagged with relevant metadata as early as possible in the workflow; this is absolutely necessary in order to enable the selection and filtering process which will lead to the aggregation of the various modules for a specific ebook.
- Create separate low-resolution and high-resolution versions of the EPUB files, for example through server-side scripting. This can also be used as a business model: offer the low-resolution book cheap or for free, and the high-resolution version for the regular price.
- For a more or less direct conversion of a print book into an electronic publication, it may be a good idea to target only one specific reading platform (in most cases: tablets), simply because the market for the publication is often limited, and because there are still major technical constraints regarding practical file sizes, download times and development costs. In this case we would recommend PDF rather than EPUB if the publication/catalogue is primarily focused on images, since PDF offers a fixed (and thus limited but easy-to-design) image layout, and can be quickly generated from an InDesign project. When cost constraints play a central role in the decision-making process, it makes sense to focus on tablets and desktop computers since these currently provide the best screen resolution, color fidelity and reading comfort for image-oriented publications. PDF is also suitable for at least some degree of interactive and multimedia content. However, such a publication should be considered a short- to medium-term product which may become technically obsolete or outmoded within three to five years. The pragmatic advice for such a rather short-lived publication is to design for a 10" tablet screen with a resolution of 1024x768 to 1920x1080 pixels, to work in InDesign, and to create if necessary a customized new page layout for these specific screen dimensions. For possible small additions of interactive and multimedia elements, consider using Adobe Acrobat Pro as a final authoring tool, but be sure to test whether the resulting PDF is also viewable in the default PDF viewing applications on iPad and Android devices.
- For a custom electronic publication which isn't conceived as a print-to-ebook conversion but rather as a modularized hybrid publishing project, EPUB is the file format of choice since it is internally modular (being a ZIP archive of individual HTML files, images, fonts

etc.). It is easy to generate an EPUB on demand from a database or a content management system (possibly in collaboration with a web developer and/or web designer) but it can be very difficult and costly to generate a high-quality PDF from the same source materials.

Some practical tips:

- Save text in the Markdown format, and make use of images in the highest resolution.
- Use a tool like Pandoc to convert the Markdown document to EPUB and to any of the other file formats you will need once the source document has been consolidated. Test the EPUB file with several e-reader devices and applications, unpack (decompress) it and adjust the HTML and CSS if necessary, and then repack (compress) it into EPUB when these customizations are done.

The step-by-step guides in the previous chapters provide a detailed description of how to use these tools.

## ARTISTS'/DESIGNERS' BOOK

There is a rich tradition of artists' audio-visual electronic books, beginning in the 1990s with hypertext and interactive multimedia literary experiments on floppy disks, CD-ROMs, websites and mobile apps. The Electronic Literature Organization[1] and the international research project ELMCIP[2] have extensively documented these historical developments. Much of this documentation can now be considered 'media archeology' since the multimedia formats have gradually become obsolete: CD-ROM applications that no longer run on contemporary computers, websites whose links or plug-ins are no longer working or no longer compatible with today's browsers, etc. This problem was actually greater in the 1990s and early 2000s, at a time when open, cross-platform multimedia standards barely existed. And yet, still today, the more complex the audio-visual materials contained in an electronic book, the less compatible it will be with various electronic reading devices, and the

1 Electronic Literature Organization, http://eliterature.org.

2 Electronic Literature Knowledge Base, http://elmcip.net/knowledgebase.

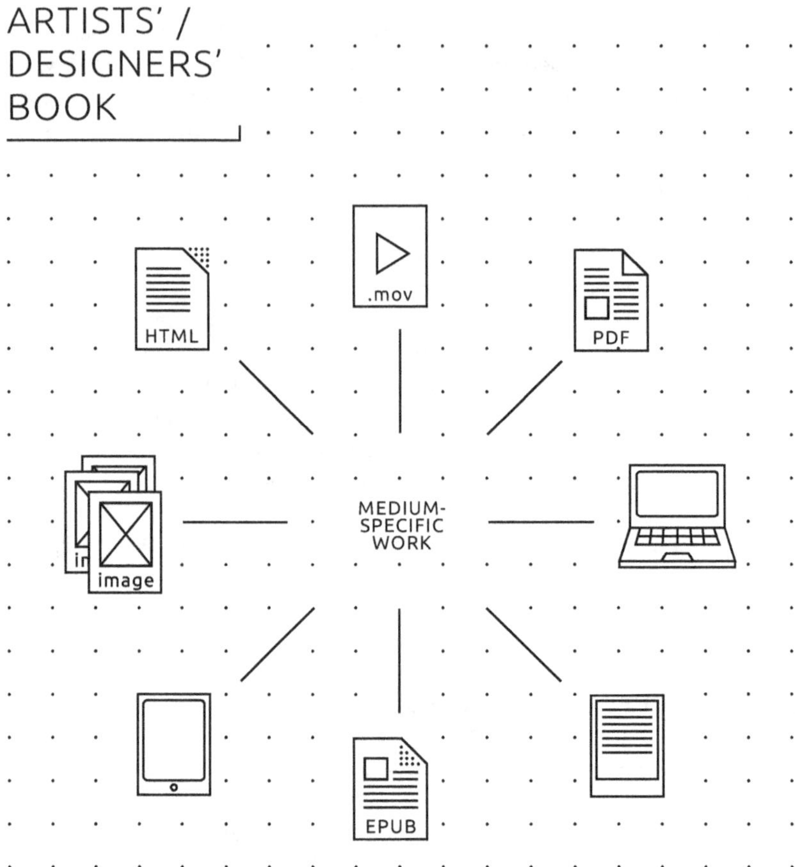


greater the number of technical updates it will likely require over the course of time. A good example of this problem is the massive use of Macromedia/ Adobe Flash by 'e-lit' artists.

More recently, artists' and designers' (print) books have grown from a niche phenomenon to a major genre within arts and design publishing. It could be argued that print books are increasingly becoming art or design objects in their own right, as electronic media is quickly replacing print as the standard carrier of generic, mundane information (such as telephone directories, dictionaries, or run-of-the-mill novels and non-fiction paperbacks). However, even before the days of the internet, artists' and designers' books were considered as conceptual design works or even sculptural objects. The more medium-specific an artists' book is, the less sense it makes to attempt to convert it one-to-one into an electronic book. For example, an electronic reproduction of Dieter Roth's sculptural book objects[3] would no longer be book artworks, but mere depictions of a book artworks.

## Workflows

Since the artists' book is not a defined genre, there is no such thing as a standard methodology or workflow. The whole spectrum of the medium can be used and experimented with. On the other hand, many contemporary artists, designers and media activists actively experiment with electronic publishing as a 'poor' (i.e. simple low-tech) medium of social sharing rather than a 'rich' visual and tactile medium; this is particularly the case in the context of artists' pirate book-sharing projects.

For artists' and designers' books that are characterized by elaborate use of typography and images, the simplest possibility is to design electronic books as a series or sequence of page-size images which can be easily converted into screen-readable PDF, EPUB and HTML5 documents. This approach would be suitable for conceptual-visual artists' books as pioneered by the Californian artist Ed Ruscha in the 1960s.[4] This would require no drastic change of workflow, and can be standardized as described in the sections on the other genres.

When creating an electronic artists'/designers' book, the editorial and design workflow – even if it is non-standard and continuously changing from one publication to the next – should nevertheless take into account the following considerations:

- Consider first the specific medium being targeted: a print book will require a completely different approach than a mobile app, a web page, an EPUB, etc.
- Depending on the final output medium, different input materials may be included or excluded.
- An artists' ebook can be based on a 'media art' approach: experiments with computer/server-generated EPUBs, use of collage and

---

3 Electronic reproduction of Dieter Roth's sculptural book objects, http://www.moma.org/visit/calendar/exhibitions/129.

4 Ed Ruscha's conceptual-visual artists' books, http://www.artnet.com/artists/ed-ruscha/.

cut-up methods, and generative art or appropriation art methodologies. (An early example is the Yes Men's appropriation of the World Trade Organization website, for which they used a self-designed software tool which automatically modified the content of the mirrored pages to suit to the Yes Men's own subversive purposes. The same could be done with electronic books.)

- An artists' blog such as those found on Tumblr can quite easily be turned into an artists' electronic book. ⦣ (*Elizabeth Castro: Catalan-Talk – Publishing multilingual interviews, from Twitter to ebooks to paper*)
- Some artists have based their work on distribution processes such as Pirate Bay-style file sharing: existing books are scanned and quickly converted into downloadable ebooks, with an emphasis on spreading and on alternative ways of networking (such as person-to-person exchange of files on flash drives).
- Electronic artists' books can be based on experimentation with existing easy-to-use authoring apps and online authoring platforms such as *The People's E-Book* or *KYUR8*.
- Proprietary authoring tools and distribution platforms such as Apple's iBooks Author can be used out of pragmatic considerations (as pioneered by Paul Chan's artists' book publishing house Badlands Unlimited). However, this will greatly limit the scope of distribution as well as the long-term readability of the project, as was the case with CD-ROM and Flash multimedia books in the past.
- Other standard file formats creatively used and abused as document formats for visual books include: animated GIF graphics files for the digital equivalent of flip books, MP4 video files displaying a book with pages that turn by themselves, MP3 audio files triggering abstract art on the volume meter display of an audio player, JPEG files with encoding artifacts of corrupted bits, etc.[5] Such files are relatively easy to create, and there are substantial communities of artists/designers actively working with such media. However, in most cases, the resulting works will only be viewable in web browsers, not on e-reader devices and applications. They also cannot be distributed through electronic bookstores.
- Self-contained HTML/HTML5; using Pandoc, it is possible to store an HTML file and all its images and style sheets as one single, large file.

5 Used as a medium of artistic experimentation among by various artists and designers, including net artists since the 1990s, and also by the conceptual poet and UbuWeb founder Kenneth Goldsmith.

Plain (ASCII) text files: these were the standard medium for self-published electronic magazines ('e-zines') and electronic 'samizdat' (Soviet hand-copied underground) books from the 1970s to the early 1990s. Since the plain-text format has remained stable since 1963, this is in fact the most resilient form of experimental electronic publishing. The website textfiles.com provides a rich archive of the plain-text electronic publishing subculture from the 1970s to the 1990s.

## ART/DESIGN PERIODICAL

Periodicals such as yearbooks and magazines are an important part of the art and culture publishing scene. Examples of influential electronic art periodicals include OPEN and e-flux . The spectrum includes everything from non-commercial websites or PDF publications, to academic and public magazines, to commercial websites and app store subscription models. At the moment, digital magazine publishing is in a process of gradually transitioning from traditional to new workflows. On a scale from traditional to new, offering a magazine as a downloadable PDF file is the most traditional solution, while turning a magazine into a website (running on a content management system such as WordPress) is the least traditional. All of these technical solutions are now finally mature after two decades of online news publishing. WordPress would be our standard recommendation for small-to-medium scale online news and journal publishing, since it is a highly developed, user-friendly, customizable and furthermore Open Source system. The main problem for publishing electronic periodicals is no longer the technology but rather the revenue model.

Aside from revenue, the main editorial question is: should the publication still be considered as *one* medium, or is it better to give up entirely on the traditional system of periodical appearance in bundled issues? Alternatively, the model could be a continuously updated website (similar to a news website or a blog), or with a focus on providing single articles rather than bundled issues, based on search engine hits, social media recommendations, etc. The difference between a 'blog' and a 'magazine', however, is becoming increasingly difficult to define.

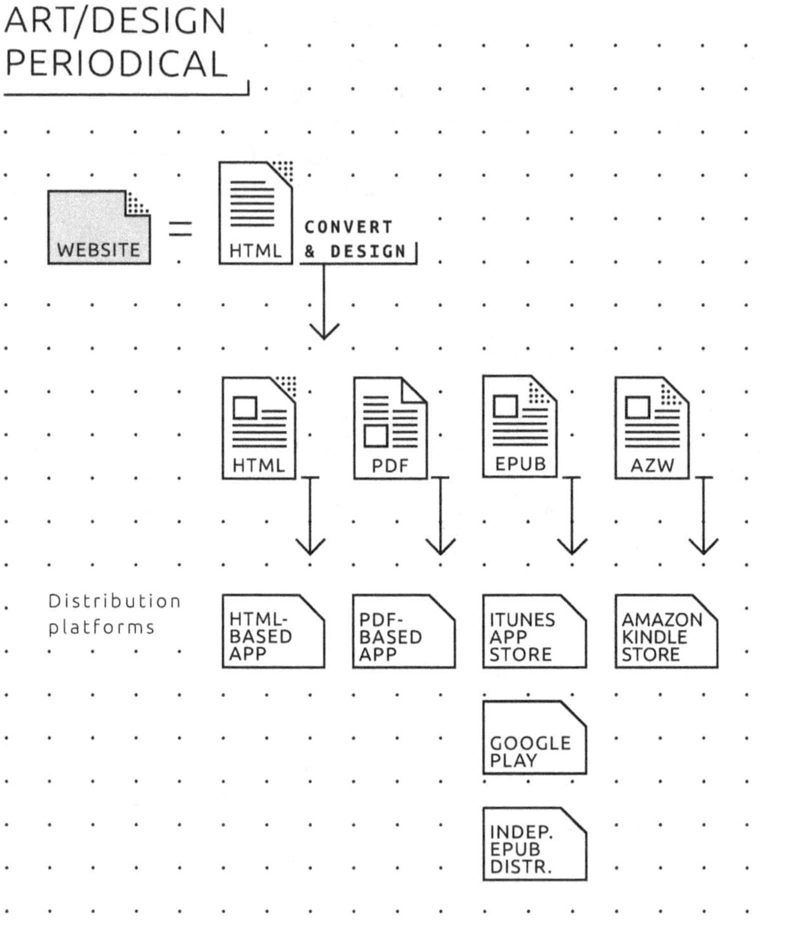


## Workflows

We distinguish between two major types of workflow, the first based on a print publication which is digitized for electronic distribution, the second based on the electronic medium itself, such as a website or blog which can make use of several distribution channels.

- Print-based workflow: The magazine is designed and put together as a print publication, using desktop publishing software such as InDesign, and exported as a printable PDF. This PDF is then optimized for reading and/or downloading on the web, meaning that the file is often smaller and the publication is distributed on different platforms which allow for online PDF reading, such as Issuu and Scribd. This provides a low-cost solution with a traditional revenue model (in-app purchase). We will not cover this field in detail here, as it is highly unstable and specific to certain countries and geographic regions. For large-scale periodicals, companies such as WoodWing offer (expensive) content management systems made for hybrid print/electronic publishing of magazines based on standard Adobe software and the PDF file format.

- HTML5-based workflow: In the Netherlands and, thanks to a strategic investment by *The New York Times*, elsewhere in the world, the Dutch electronic news platform Blendle is currently gaining ground as an 'iTunes for newspapers and magazines'. It serves as an electronic newsstand where readers can purchase access to whole issues or single articles of all major newspapers and magazines available in their country, and is run as an open, publisher-neutral platform. It remains to be seen whether this model will provide a viable solution for smaller publishers or for selling (articles from) art periodicals. At the moment, it is too early to offer any practical recommendations on this subject. Currently, only small numbers of readers in the field of arts, design and culture are likely to be users of apps such as Blendle.

- Web-based workflow: The magazine is a self-published website. There are many ways of building websites, but the easiest Open Source, free solution is to use a content management system like WordPress with a custom design template for your own publication. This allows you to have a responsive design that adapts to all available reading devices. An additional technical benefit is that this workflow allows you to have a structured database of everything ever published on the site, which is easy to use as a basis for exporting to custom publications such as downloadable ebooks, InDesign layout for print yearbooks, PDFs, a tablet app, etc.

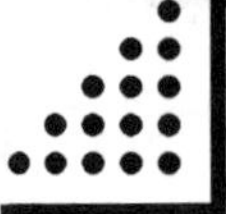

# 09 FUTUROLOGY

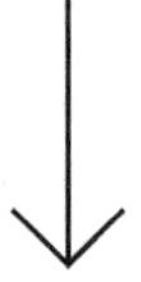

- Customization and curation seem to be key concepts in electronic publishing for the future.
- Traditional e-readers appear to be losing market share, with more and more people reading on their standard mobile devices.
- Electronic reading and paper publications will in all likelihood continue to coexist.
- Flat-rate subscriptions to entire catalogues of ebooks will likely become more common, seriously disrupting today's publishing and library culture.
- Self-publishing is likely to go on increasing.
- As a consequence, there will probably be an increased need for editorial selection and content curation.

Throughout the 20th century, new art forms and mass media have often been closely interrelated. For example, it is almost impossible to consider Cubist, Dadaist and Pop Art collage outside the context of a mass culture of newspaper publishing. With the advent of electronic publishing, the practices of dissecting, copy-pasting and perpetually reorganizing have become technologically and culturally more complex – as well as more common. In this Toolkit, we have referred to such processes as the 'modularization' of electronic publishing. Personalized, individually curated, or 'collaged' content can be done both on the side of the producer and of the receiver. Furthermore, users can choose their own combinations of reading technologies. There is no reason to believe that the current diversity of reading software and hardware is going to decrease. Indeed, perhaps it will increase even further – contrary to expectations from only five years ago, when many believed that Apple's iPad would establish a unified standard for electronic reading devices.

Is it possible then to make a few general statements about the future of electronic publishing? We can distinguish some real trends, though of course predictions are always questionable in a field so prone to fashions and hypes. ⊾ (*The End of Ebooks. 20 Visionaries on the Future of Digital Reading*)

## TECHNOLOGY

Reading novels and other conventional texts on e-reader devices is already a common practice, and the technology is clearly an industry success. Publishers report ever-increasing sales of ebooks. It is quite possible that someday soon, sales of electronic publications will surpass those of paper publications.[1]

At the same time, the market for e-reading devices is increasingly showing signs of saturation. Early mass producers of monochrome e-readers such as Sony have dropped out of this market, so that the further development of these devices is left to smaller companies such as Kobo. This may to a large extent be a result of the popularity of tablets and smartphones. Since smartphones are sold with increasingly large screens, we are already seeing signs

1 Digital sales outstrip bricks and mortar in US, http://www.thebookseller.com/news/digital-sales-outstrip-bricks-and-mortar-us.

of a convergence between these two types of devices. It is quite possible to read comfortably from a large smartphone, with the added advantage that people already carry their phones on them, always and everywhere. Generally speaking, and beyond the relatively narrow field of ebooks, it is fair to assume that at least in Western and East Asian countries, most people spend more time reading on electronic devices than they do on print.

Ongoing technological development of higher-quality screens is, at least for the time being, a never-ending process: color e-paper screens, Ultra High Density (4K) resolution, even flexible displays. However, recent research shows that students preparing for tests and exams still prefer paper to electronic displays.[2] In the field of educational texts, we are already seeing new combinations of paper textbooks and electronic materials (such as image, audio and film collections, and interactive tests and exams) that are written and developed to complement each other. Where paper publications are used for reading complex texts, (portable) electronic devices will simultaneously be used for purposes of searching and meta-tagging, and for commenting and debating on the content.

Presumably, all these developments will also find their way into areas outside the world of education. It remains to be seen whether 'social reading' – which includes social practices of browsing, annotating, sharing and quoting – will really take off for ebooks, or whether this will remain the domain of 'traditional' social media such as Facebook, Twitter and Reddit. So far, the efforts in this respect by established players like Kobo and startups like Sobooks have not lived up to expectations.

The impact and value of digital libraries, with their extensive collections and their specific advantages of affordability and portability, can hardly be overstated. However this gain also comes at a price: dependence on electricity, and loss of the visual and tactile qualities of paper books. Arguably, electronic and print publishing are currently developing into opposite directions precisely because of their opposite qualities of affordability/portability vs. tangibility. As electronic books – integrated into vast digital libraries – gradually replace generic text books such as paperbacks, printed books may well

2 Judith Stoop, Paulien Kreutzer, and Joost Kircz. 'Reading and Learning from Screens versus Print: a study in changing habits. Part 1 – reading long information rich texts', New Library World, Vol. 114, Issue 7/8, pp. 284-300, 2013. 'Part 2 – comparing different text structures on paper and on screen', New Library World, Vol. 114, Issue 9/10, pp. 371-383, 2013.

become valuable design objects rather than cheap throwaway mass media, eventually occupying a similar 'craft' niche as calligraphy after the invention of the printing press, and letterpress typesetting after the invention of photo-typesetting.

But where will these electronic libraries be stored, and who will control access to them? The 'cloud' is entirely dependent on a permanent supply of electricity, on a dense and fast internet infrastructure, and on hardware/software platform consistency. Who will guarantee that the cloud, containing all your books and other data, will be perpetually maintained, kept open and accessible – let alone unfiltered and free from surveillance and censorship?

## READING AND BOOK CULTURE

In reading culture and book retail, we can already see a shift from buying and owning individual ebooks towards all-you-can-read subscription models. Just like the music and film industries before them (with Spotify and Netflix respectively), the publishing industry is moving towards flat-rate subscription packages. In the U.S., Oyster Books offers a 'streaming service' for books, while Amazon has recently launched its Kindle Unlimited program, with access to 600,000 ebooks for a monthly fee of $10. Such services have major drawbacks: the books they offer are no longer stored on people's devices, but only accessed from a remote server. Therefore they are subject to arbitrary modifications, censorship or even outright deletion. These books will disappear as soon as the central server disappears – which can happen overnight. The same economic pressures that are currently forcing the industry to lower the price of ebooks, may well end up disempowering readers.

The commerce of publishing will also be increasingly advertisement-driven. Statistical data-mining of consumer habits, as already practiced by Facebook, Google and Amazon, will of course influence consumers' choices. This model is likely to become the norm once subscription models are widely adopted. Then user statistics and 'big data' will be at the heart of the publishing industry's business models.

Flat-rate ebook subscriptions will eventually pose a serious threat to today's public libraries. Such new models offer attractive cost-cutting opportunities for policy makers. After transportation, energy, arts and education, public libraries could be the next on the list of public services and infrastructure that will be subject to sweeping neo-liberal budget cuts. On the other hand, the new electronic libraries will help level the global playing field of higher education: first-class research libraries will then no longer be the exclusive domain of traditional, highly-funded, Western universities.

How will people read in the future? Do people read ebooks from the beginning to the end, or do they casually browse them – or merely keep them as searchable items in a personal electronic library? Do they read PDF versions of books and articles on display screens, or do they first print them on paper? How much content is read only by internet bots and search engines? Will attention spans decrease (the age-old criticism of any new medium)? Or will long, complex texts and printed books become fashionable again in a more mature technological environment? It is very possible that in the course of time, users will adjust to the new reading technologies, and have no trouble digesting long and complex texts from the displays of their mobile devices.

## THE FUTURE OF PUBLISHING CULTURE?

Already today, increasing numbers of writers and artists self-publish their works. For them, print-on-demand (POD) publication often fills a gap between traditional and electronic publishing.[3] The role of publishers as book producers is rapidly becoming a thing of the past. However, at a certain point of overproduction and oversaturation, publishers may redefine their role to become aggregators and curators. A new publishing house like Zero Books (featuring authors who mostly belong to a small, carefully selected group of critical theory bloggers) demonstrates that this model already works today. In the meantime, sales platforms like Amazon have become too large to provide a competitive level of selection and curatorship; even their statistics-driven customer personalization has not yet proven successful in this respect.

3 Take for example the 528 page (and 10.8 x 17.48 cm) thick anthology What will be / Ce qui sera / Lo que será Almanac on the international Surrealist movement, with more than 170 contributors from 25 countries: essays, poems, images, manifestos, a debate on Surrealist editions, a chronology of 50 years of Surrealism from 1964 to 2014. Downloading such a book is problematic due to the need of a complete structured index and advanced search options. Printing it locally is almost impossible because of its small fixed-page size. Buying it at lulu.com gives readers a print-on-demand book on standard glossy paper which is certainly not in line with the Surrealist tradition.

The electronic publishing models which we have focused on in this Toolkit, using technologies such as EPUB, may in some cases appear counter-intuitive to today's digital media culture: why create what are essentially offline websites in ZIP files, in this age of 'cloud computing' and an 'always-on' culture in which we are constantly connected and networked? However, it is precisely the ephemeral nature of networked media that makes a format like EPUB increasingly attractive. As an offline, stable medium based on World Wide Web technology, it is perfect for everyone who wishes to personally curate, collect and preserve what otherwise may soon be lost.[4]

Faced with on one hand all these new possibilities for self-publishing and self-curating, and on the other hand the rise and consolidation of huge commercial monopolies, the art and craftsmanship of publishing will have no choice but to reinvent and rebuild itself. Through this Toolkit, we hope to contribute to at least one of the building blocks of this process.

4 See also Henry Warwick, *Radical Tactics of the Offline Library,* Network Notebooks No. 07, Amsterdam; Institute of Network Cultures, 2014.

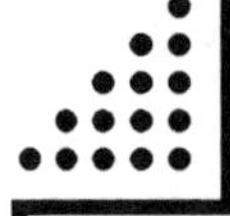

# 10 SOFTWARE CATALOGUE

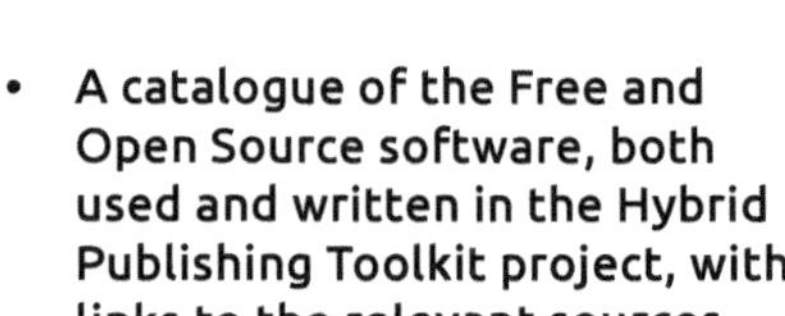

- A catalogue of the Free and Open Source software, both used and written in the Hybrid Publishing Toolkit project, with links to the relevant sources.

### CakePHP

A piece of web developer software that makes it easy to create web-based applications in the programming language PHP.

http://cakephp.org/

### epubtrailer.py

A small program written in the Python programming language that automatically generates a visual book trailer from an EPUB file, in the form of an animated (GIF) image.

https://github.com/DigitalPublishingToolkit/epubtrailer.py

### EPUBster

A web application for creating and editing EPUBs, written in CakePHP.

https://github.com/DigitalPublishingToolkit/epubster

### expand_toc.py

A small program written in the Python programming language to generate a table of contents for an EPUB that has been created from a Markdown document file.

https://github.com/DigitalPublishingToolkit/Society-of-the-Query-Reader/blob/master/scripts/expand_toc.py

### Git

Git is a distributed version control system created for collaborative software development. Similar to popular applications like Dropbox and Google Drive, it allows users to share folders on their computer with others, synchronizing the changes made by different users the files in those folders. Unlike Dropbox or Google Drive however, it stores all previous versions of edited files and automatically resolves inconsistencies when two people edit different parts of the same file. Such shared Git folders may be put on a public website such as GitHub or Gitorious, or on a private server. Git is not owned by any company, but is Open Source / Free Software. It was created by the inventor of Linux, Linus Torvalds, is widely used all over the world, and is a very reliable piece of software.

http://git-scm.com/

### ICML

ICML is the file format of InCopy, Adobe's word processor built into InDesign. With the application Pandoc, Markdown files can be easily converted into ICML, preserving the logical structure of the document. The resulting file can then be imported into InDesign and be used as the basis of a print design. See the related blog post on Make and its use in one of our projects.

### Make

The GNU Make program helps to automate workflows in which a number of command-line programs and scripts need to be repeatedly used, for example when converting documents. Instead of running a number of such scripts by hand one after another, Make allows to run them in a single batch while applying predefined rules and conditions for this process. See the related blog post on how Make has been used in one of our projects. A Makefile can be seen as a kind of a developer's notebook that helps organize one's toolbox of scripts. Make is Open Source / Free Software.

http://www.gnu.org/software/make/

### Markdown

Markdown is a simple structured text format. It was originally designed to allow writers to use informal, human-readable formatting in blog posts, using writing conventions found in plain-text emails and chats, rather than reader-unfriendly and writer-unfriendly HTML code. Though it originated from the blogging and coding communities, Markdown is gaining popularity and is supported by a wide range of tools and programs (See Mou below). This blog post compares Markdown with HTML in the context of one of our own e-book development projects. Most Markdown tools are Open Source / Free Software, and the format is currently in the process of becoming an open standard.

http://daringfireball.net/projects/markdown/

### mmd-meta-validation

A simple validation tool for checking metadata in a Markdown file.

https://github.com/DigitalPublishingToolkit/mmd-meta-validation

### My Highlights

Our project for nai010 Publishers included two technical components. The first is a mobile web application, called My Highlights, which allows a user to browse a large collection and create an EPUB based on a personal selection of catalogue texts on art works from the collection of the Stedelijk Museum Amsterdam. The other is a set of plug-ins for the popular web content management system WordPress, extending the functionality of the WordPress JSON REST application programming interface (API) (WP-AP)[1] and facilitating the generation of EPUBs directly from a WordPress database. (The latter is for the most part a packaged version of the CakePHP EPUB component that builds on Asbjørn Grandt's PHPePub.)

https://github.com/DigitalPublishingToolkit/my-highlights

---

1 A JSON-based REST API for WordPress, https://github.com/WP-API/WP-API.

### Pandoc

Pandoc is the 'Swiss-army knife' of text converters, an Open Source software application able to convert between a wide variety of document formats. In our projects, Pandoc has been the essential tool for converting documents written in Microsoft Word to Markdown, and then later for converting edited Markdown source documents to EPUB. Pandoc only has a command-line interface and can be run in the Mac OS X Terminal, the Windows Command Prompt and the Linux Terminal. The program has an enormous amount of features such as user-defined design templates and metadata management. It can be used for all kinds of purposes and can be highly customized for one's particular document creation needs. Our Hybrid Workflow How-To Guides (for editors, designers, and developers include various real-world examples for using Pandoc.

http://johnmacfarlane.net/pandoc/

### PHPePub

For Valiz Publishers, an online EPUB generator was developed based on CakePHP and a set of Open Source software modules, notably Asbjørn Grandt's PHPePub.[2] The project was developed with relatively low-cost and low-feature[3] web hosting in mind. Notable features include support for endnotes and a WYSIWYG editor based on HTML5's 'content-editable' mechanism. The platform allows publishers to author and generate EPUBs suitable for distribution in various bookstores.

https://github.com/Grandt/PHPePub

### PHP

PHP is a programming language typically coupled with a web server and used for creating dynamic websites.

http://php.net

### Python

Python is a general-purpose programming (or scripting) language. In one of our projects, Python was used to make small 'helper' programs to clean up HTML, to extract and accumulate metadata from different files, and to create animated GIF book trailers from EPUB files. Python scripts often make use of additional program modules known as libraries. For our project, we made use of the html-5lib and images2gif libraries. Python is Free Software / Open Source and comes pre-installed on Mac OS X and all standard flavors of Linux. For all other operating systems, an installer can be downloaded from the Python website.

http://www.python.org/

---

2 Asbjørn Grandt's PHPePub, https://github.com/Grandt/PHPePub.

3 E.g. no command-line access, limited possibilities for executing external programs like Pandoc.

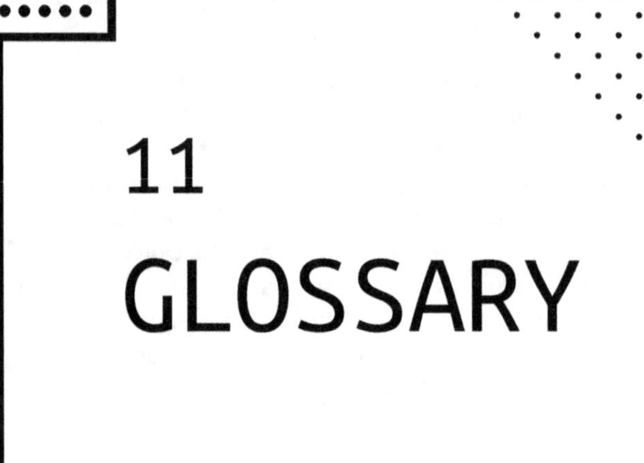

# 11 GLOSSARY

# A

## Acronym

An acronym is a shortened version of a phrase, often based on the first letter of each word. For example, WYSIWYG is the acronym for 'What You See Is What You Get'. Some acronyms use more than one letter from each word (or omit some words), for example EPUB is an acronym for Electronic PUBlication.

## Amazon

A well-known online retailer of various goods, including print books and ebooks. Amazon also produces the Kindle e-reader devices.

## Anchor

An anchor is a specific location within a HTML web page or other hypertext document that can be jumped to, for example by clicking on a hyperlink.

## Android

Google's operating system for mobile phones and tablets, based on the Linux kernel and the Java programming language. Android is currently the most widely used operating system for mobile devices (including smartphones and tablets).

## Animated GIF

A graphic file format consisting of two or more image frames shown as moving images in a timed sequence; most often used for endlessly looping mini-films or graphic animations that only last a few seconds. (GIF is an acroym for Graphics Interchange Format.)

## App store

An online store where applications may be bought or obtained for free. Every major mobile operating system also has its own app store: App Store (Apple), Google Play, Amazon Appstore, Windows Phone Store and BlackBerry World.

## Application or app

See Software. The word 'app' was originally a marketing term invented by Apple to win over resistance against installing third-party software on the iPhone. Nowadays, the word is most commonly used for (usually relatively small) software applications running on mobile or desktop operating systems and which are downloaded and installed from an app store.

## Application Programming Interface (API)

A standardized way for software applications to communicate with each other and use each other's resources. APIs are used in software development; end users normally do not see them.

## ASCII

American Standard Code for Information Interchange: the standard encoding format for plain-text files in English since 1963. ASCII is limited to 128 characters and therefore excludes diacritic (accented) characters and non-European writing systems. For written text, ASCII has therefore been superseded by Unicode (which can store characters of practically every writing system). ASCII text remains the standard format for programming and markup languages. See also Unicode.

### AZW

Presumably an acronym for 'Amazon Word'. A file format used by Amazon for its Kindle range of e-reader devices and software applications. See also KF8 and MOBI.

# B

### Bandwidth

The physical transmission capacity of a communication channel. Often used as an expression of the maximum amount of data that can be sent via a specific network connection. The higher the bandwidth, the greater the amount of data that can be transmitted within a given time period. Bandwidth is therefore crucial for services such as video streaming (where playback would stop if the bandwidth were too low to transmit the data quickly enough).

### Binary

A numeral system based on only two values, zero and one. For example, the binary representation of the number 9 is 1001. Because of the straightforward implementation of binary numbers in electronic circuits, all computing devices are ultimately based on this numeral system.

### Bit

Contraction of 'binary digit'. A bit is the smallest measurement unit of computer memory or processing, or data transmission speed. The binary code '1001', for example, consists of four bits. See also Binary.

### BitTorrent

BitTorrent is the most popular internet technology for file sharing and downloading large amounts of data (such as movies). It works according to a principle known as 'peer-to-peer', which means that everyone who is downloading a file is simultaneously uploading it to fellow downloaders. This way, bandwidth is shared among the downloaders, and no central download server is necessary.

### Blog

Short for 'web log'; usually a chronological and often personal record of thoughts, web links, events or actions, posted on the web. The difference between blogs and news/opinion websites is becoming increasingly blurry.

### Browser

The software used by people for accessing and viewing websites. A web browser loads pages from servers, translates their internal HTML code into formatted text, displays graphics, plays music and video, and provides links to related pages. Web browsers are based on the file format and network standards of the World Wide Web, which are defined by the World Wide Web Consortium. In practice, however, browser manufacturers extend or deviate from those standards, which can lead to compatibility problems in web design.

### Browser extension

Plug-ins (additional software modules) which extend or enhance the inner workings of a web browser.

# C

## Cascading Style Sheets (CSS)

Cascading Style Sheets are a markup language for formatting electronic text with typographical attributes (such as bold, italic, font type, font size, color, margins, etc.). CSS is most commonly used for (HTML) web pages, and by extension also for EPUB. CSS is typically stored in a separate file so that the content and the visual layout of a document remain separated from each other. Cascading Style Sheets make it easy to design a typographic template for a whole website or ebook. In order to change the typography, one only needs to edit the CSS file. Also, by using different CSS files for the same document, it also is easy to define formattings for different purposes without having to modify the document itself.

## Compatibility

Pieces of hardware and/or software which work together are called compatible. Conversely, if they do not work together, they are incompatible. For example, Android and iOS are incompatible because Android apps do not work under iOS and vice versa.

## Compressed files

Compression is a technique for shrinking the size of a file or a data stream. As a result it can be transmitted faster, and will take up less storage space on a device. For example, digital video is heavily compressed, otherwise it would not fit on a DVD and could not be streamed over internet connections. Another example is EPUB, which consists of a compressed collection of HTML files. Various software applications such as PKZIP, WinZip, 7zip, Stuffit, GNU gzip/tar, and many others, can compress a set of files into single-file archives, and decompress the archive back to separate files. Files with the following extensions are almost always compressed file collections: epub, tar.gz/tgz, rar and zip.

## Content Management System (CMS)

Software that makes it possible to publish and manage content (text, images, etc.) on a website without having to manually create HTML files. For example, practically all blogs and all shopping websites are based on content management systems. Most content management systems use internal databases to store their information (such as blog articles or sales items). Content management systems automatically generate a web page 'on the fly' from their database contents when the page is requested by a user. See also Server-side scripting.

# D

## Data

In the context of computing, data is simply any kind of information that is stored and processed on a computing device. Generally a distinction is made between data and software: software processes data, and conversely data is processed by software (for example: a graphics software application for manipulating an image). A computer or mobile device is, in the end, simply a machine that uses software to process data. See also Software.

### Database

An organized, structured collection of information: common examples are address books, library catalogues and retail inventories. A database consists of entries called 'records' (for example, each record could be one person's name and address), and these records are broken down into 'fields' (such as: first name, last name, street, postal code, city, etc.). This rigorous structure makes it easy to select specific subsets of information from the database based on specific search criteria (for example: select and show all people whose last name is Mulder and who live in Amsterdam).

### Dataset

A dataset (or data set) is, as the word suggests, a collection of data – typically, a number of entries extracted from a database based on specific search criteria. For example: from an address database of all residents of Amsterdam, one could extract a dataset of all residents living in a particular neighborhood, and store the results in a new file.

### Desktop Publishing (DTP)

The design of printed matter on a personal computer using graphical What-You-See-Is-What-You-Get (WYSIWYG) software such as Adobe InDesign or QuarkXPress. DTP software uses a graphical user interface to visually simulate the analog layout desks used in pre-digital times by graphic and editorial designers.

### Device

In the context of mobile computing, a device is an electronic handheld gadget such as a smartphone, tablet, phablet (large-screen smartphone) or portable gaming device.

### Digital Rights Management (DRM)

Technology used by publishers to restrict the usage and copying of copyright-protected digital materials (audio and video files, e-books, games, etc.). The practice of adding DRM to media is controversial, as it often obstructs paying customers from making full use of the digital goods they have purchased. For example, most files with DRM cannot be freely transferred between two devices owned by the same user. Also, it is often not possible to even access these files without an active internet connection. Finally, DRM is a major obstacle for long-term storage and accessibility of digital media.

## E

### Ebook

A digital publication which can be read on e-readers and other handheld devices, as well as desktop computers. Unlike online digital publications (such as news websites and blogs), most ebooks are meant for offline reading and individual collecting. There are various ebook formats such as EPUB and AZW, most of which are based on web design technologies such as HTML and CSS.

### EPUB

Acronym for Electronic Publication. An ebook format developed by the International Digital Publishing Forum (IDPF). EPUB is an open standard and the most commonly used and supported file format for electronic books. EPUB was designed to accommodate reflowable content. See also Reflowable.

### E-paper

Electronic paper, a display technology designed to resemble printed paper rather than the LCD displays used on most other computing devices. E-paper consists of a grid of tiny electronic 'ink' particles that can be switched from black to white. Electricity is only needed for refreshing ('turning') the page; for the display itself, no electricity or battery power is needed. Since it is not backlit like an LCD, the display must be illuminated externally like conventional paper; the upside is that it can be read in broad daylight without any loss of image quality. Since the refresh rate is much slower than LCD screens, the technology does not allow for videos or animations. See also LCD.

### E-reader

A device capable of displaying digital texts in various formats, notably EPUB, or in the case of Amazon's Kindle e-readers, Amazon's own proprietary formats AZW, KF8 and MOBI. Many e-readers also support PDF and other formats.

# F

### File

A file is an object containing data and metadata, and stored on a computer, server or mobile device. A file can contain a text, an image, a video, a software program, etc. On most computer systems, files are organized within hierarchies of folders.

### Filename extension

A filename extension typically consists of three or four letters at the end of a filename, preceded by a dot (such as: .html, .mp4, .jpg/.jpeg, etc.). Filename extensions are used by many operating systems including Windows and Mac OS X to indicate the type of a file.

### Folder

On most operating systems, files are grouped and hierarchically organized in folders. The term 'folder' is used synonymously with 'directory'. Folders can be hierarchically organized in a tree-like structure, so that one folder contains a number of other folders, each of which may contain yet more folders, etc. Subfolders are sometimes referred to as 'child folders' of the 'parent folder'.

### Formatting

The process of applying typographic styling (bold, italic, etc.) to a text. Another unrelated meaning of the same term is: to erase and initialize a storage device (such as a hard disk or memory card).

### Freemium

A revenue model in which the basic product or service (typically software, media, games or web services) is provided free of charge, but money (a premium) is charged for extra features or virtual goods.

# G

### GitHub

A freemium web hosting service for user-run Git repositories. Git, an Open Source software application for collaborative editing over the internet, is described in our software catalogue.

### Graphical User Interface (GUI)

Software that allows human users to use a computer or other digital device in a visual-tactile way, as opposed to text-based command-line interfaces, and typically creating the 'look and feel' of a tangible physical instrument. A GUI features graphical elements such as menus, icons, pointers, check boxes, knobs, dials and sliders. By clicking and dragging these elements, the user can run and control software programs and carry out other operations such as copying information, deleting files, etc.

## H

### HTML (Hypertext Markup Language)

A file format and markup standard used mainly for web pages. HTML consists of ASCII files with markup tags in angular brackets, like this: <tag>. These tags allow the author or designer to define the structural document layout (such as the title, headlines, block quotes, lists, tables) and interaction elements (such as hyperlinks and fill-out forms).

### HTML5

The most recent version of the HTML format. HTML5 adds various new features, notably support for the multimedia (audio and video) capabilities of the World Wide Web. Through the adoption of HTML5, web designers hope to render obsolete the use of browser plug-ins for interactive multimedia websites.

### Hybrid Publishing

Hybrid publishing, also known as multi-channel publishing, means the publishing of a single publication in several different print and electronic media, preferably with a workflow that minimizes the effort of customizing the publication for each medium.

### Hyperlink

A hyperlink (hypertext link) is a clickable cross-reference between electronic documents. By clicking a hyperlink, the user is led to another part of the document, or to a different document, web page or website. Hyperlinks are usually highlighted and/or underlined so that users can easily recognize them in the text.

### Hypertext

A system for the non-linear organization of text, and arguably the fundamental underlying principle of the World Wide Web. The concept of hypertext predates the web by many years.

## I

### iBooks

A software application which allows users to purchase, read and manage ebooks. Developed by Apple for its iOS and Mac OS X operating systems.

### Icon

A small symbol or picture used in a graphical user interface (GUI). The icons on the computer screen visually represent software programs or data files. For example, a picture of a painter's palette may be used to represent software used for drawing and editing pictures, and a picture of a book with a question mark on its cover may represent the text of a user manual or a help file.

### Interactivity

In the context of computer engineering, the ways in which software accepts and responds to user input. In other words, a system is considered 'interactive' if it reacts to human input.

### Internet

The internet is the global computer network connecting billions of computers all over the world (through the network protocol TCP/IP). The internet dates back to a group of interconnected computer networks in U.S. universities in the late 1960s and early 1970s. Contrary to popular belief, the World Wide Web (with its hypertext pages) is *not* the internet, but just one service running on top of it. (Others include e-mail, BitTorrent, and voice-over-IP services such as Skype.)

### iOS

Apple's mobile operating system for the iPhone, iPad, iPod Touch and Apple TV.

## J

### JavaScript

JavaScript is a relatively simple, special-purpose programming language for running small programs directly on web pages, within the web browser. JavaScript is very popular for common tasks such as checking whether all fields of a web form have been filled in, or for building websites that behave like software applications (such as web mail services). Despite its name, JavaScript is unrelated to the more complex programming language Java.

### JPEG

Acronym for Joint Photographic Experts Group, and also known as JPG. JPEG is a file format used for digital images, and particularly suitable for photographs and full-color artworks. The JPEG format has a rich color palette of millions of colors, but it also compresses data through reduction of visual details, resulting in a loss of image quality. In practice however, this loss of quality is often invisible to the human eye.

## K

### KF8

KF8 is the latest ebook format used by Amazon for its Kindle range of e-reader devices. Like EPUB3, it is internally based on HTML5. See also AZW and MOBI.

### Kindle

Amazon's Kindle is a range of handheld e-reader devices and companion software applications for reading ebooks, particularly in Amazon's proprietary AZW, KF8 and MOBI ebook formats.

### Kobo

Kobo is a company that produces a range of handheld e-reader devices and companion software. It also has its own online store where users can purchase ebooks (mainly in the EPUB format).

# L

## LaTeX

A document markup language in use since the 1980s, mainly for typesetting scientific documents. LaTeX is particularly useful for rendering complex mathematical formulas.

## Layout

The overall visual design of a document. In the case of printed matter, layout includes elements such as page dimensions and margins, font type and size, markup formatting, the placement of various elements within the page, and various other elements such as headings and page numbers. In the case of reflowable documents such as ebooks, the layout is dynamically adapted to each screen size and screen aspect ratio.

## LCD

Acronym for Liquid Crystal Display. The technology used for producing the flat-panel color display screens found on most contemporary computers, tablets and smartphones, as well as a variety of other devices. TFT (Thin Film Transistor) LCD displays are the most common type of display today, so that the term 'TFT' is often used interchangeably with 'LCD'. See also E-paper.

## Linux

A popular Open Source, Unix-compatible operating system. Linux is named after its creator Linus Torvalds, who still supervises its development by many developers worldwide. Most web servers today run Linux. Google's Android operating system is also based on Linux. (Unix, originally developed in the early 1970, is also the foundation of other operating systems such as Mac OS X and iOS.)

# M

## Markdown

A simple markup language for plain-text files which uses common, easily readable symbols such as #, * and _ to define document formatting. Markdown was originally developed for blogs, as a quick and easy way of writing texts that would be eventually be converted into HTML. Nowadays, Markdown can also be converted to other document formats including EPUB. See also the more powerful extension of Markdown, MultiMarkdown.

## Markup

Symbols/codes inserted in a text document in order to define additional attributes such as formatting instructions (bold, italics, etc.), structuring instructions (chapters, headings, references, etc.) or metadata. Based on the information contained in the markup code, software applications can render the text document for a specific output medium (such as a screen or print).

## Markup language

A document format consisting of a clearly defined syntax of markup codes. Markup languages are typically created for specific purposes: For example, HTML and CSS for formatting web pages, LaTeX for scientific typesetting.

**Metadata**

Literally: data about data. Metadata contains general descriptions of the data contained within a particular document. For example: if a book is data, then a library index card for that book is its metadata.

**MOBI**

An ebook file format developed by Mobipocket, and the basis of Amazon's earliest AZW ebooks for the Kindle e-reader.

**Mobipocket**

A French company founded in 2000 that produced Mobipocket Reader, an e-reader software application that ran on some handheld computers, wireless telephones and desktop operating systems. The technology was later purchased by Amazon for its Kindle platform.

**Monitor**

The screen on which the output from a computer is displayed. Also referred to as display screen.

**Monochrome**

Monochrome images are either in one color (black and white) or shades of one color (grayscale).

**MP3**

Acronym for 'MPEG-1 or MPEG-2 Audio Layer III'. A common compression format for digital audio. MP3 shrinks audio files to a fraction of their original size. The technology was developed in the 1990s and has not (yet) been superseded by newer and technically superior compression formats such as MP4 AAC.

**MP4**

Also known as MPEG-4. A common compression format for digital video (MP4 AVC) and audio (MP4 AAC). The MP4 AAC audio format is the default audio format for Apple's iPod, iPhone and iPad devices and iTunes store. MP4 AVC is currently the standard video compression format for BluRay, digital TV, internet video (on YouTube, Vimeo, Netflix, etc.), mobile devices and consumer video cameras.

**MultiMarkdown**

An extension of the markup language Markdown, with additional support for footnotes, tables, mathematical formulas, cross-references, bibliographies and definition lists.

**Multimedia**

The integration of two or more media (text, images, audio, video, animation, etc.) in a single document or software application.

**Open Source**

Open Source originally refers to software that can be freely used, copied, adapted and modified. In order to allow modification, Open Source software provides users and developers not only with the installable software, but also its human-readable 'source' code. (An analogy would be a restaurant where customers can not only order dishes, but are also given the cooking recipes for unrestricted – personal as well as commercial – reuse.) The term has also been used to describe similar practices in fields other than software development, such as design (Open Design), publishing (Open Access), engineering, and even medical research.

### Operating system

The most basic piece of software running on a computer. Operating systems generally manage storage and file access as well as network connectivity, and provide a user interface including keyboard/mouse input and screen/audio output. Well-known operating systems include Windows, Linux and Mac OS X, as well as mobile operating systems such as Android and iOS.

### Optical Character Recognition (OCR)

OCR software automatically recognizes printed text (or even handwriting) in scanned or photographed images and converts it into digital text files.

## P

### PDA (Personal Digital Assistant)

A miniature computer/handheld device with standard software applications such as an agenda, address book, notebook and web browsing. PDAs were popular from the 1990s to the mid-2000s, when they were superseded by smartphones.

### PDF

Acronym for Portable Document Format. PDF was developed by Adobe Systems as a file format for ensuring that documents would retain their visual layout and typographic details, and thus be rendered identically, across all operating systems. PDF is generally a read-only format, and not a suitable format for editable documents. It originated in the field of desktop publishing and became the standard file format for master copies of print publications. Since PDF is, for the most part, a fixed-layout (as opposed to reflowable) document format, designed for print, it is less suitable than EPUB as an all-purpose electronic publishing format. Since 2008, PDF has been an open standard.

### Pixel

All text and images on a display screen are made up of a grid of thousands (or even millions) of small colored dots known as pixels. The term 'pixel' is derived from 'picture element'. See also Resolution.

### Plain text

Text without any visual formatting (such as bold, italic, font types and sizes, clickable hyperlinks, etc.). ASCII is the oldest and still most common plain-text format.

### Platform

A generic term to describe technology that serves as a foundation for other technology. For example, the internet is a platform for other network services, and operating systems are platforms for other software applications. (Platform-independent software can, theoretically, run on any computer.)

### Print-on-demand (POD)

Print-on-demand (POD) is a digital printing technology in which a book or other publication is not printed in an edition of several hundred or thousand copies, but in individual copies 'on demand' based on a single customer's order. The emergence of POD has had a significant impact on the publishing industry, as it allowed authors for the first time to self-publish at a very low cost. Print-on-demand is sometimes also called publishing on demand.

### Program

The terms program, software, application and app are often used more or less interchangeably. A program tells a computer or mobile device what to do. Programs are usually written in 'high-level' programming languages (such as C, C++, Java, Python) which are a mixture of English-language commands and mathematical-logical expressions. See also Software.

### Protocol

In computing and networking, a protocol is a technical standard according to which two systems communicate with each other. For example, the HTTP protocol defines the format for communication between web browsers and web servers. (Or, to use an 'old media' example: frequency modulation (FM) is the technical protocol for most radio transmissions.)

## R

### Reflowable

A reflowable document is a document without a predefined page layout, in which the page dimensions are dynamically and automatically adapted (including page breaks) to each screen size and screen aspect ratio. This means, for example, that an ebook may appear as 50 A5-size pages on a tablet, but as 100 A6-size pages on an e-reader. This also means that the designer no longer has control of the final page layout. The concept is also known as 'responsive design'.

### Resolution

The smaller a pixel, the higher the visual resolution of any display. Resolution is commonly expressed as the number of dots per square inch (dpi) of a printed output or display. For digital print the industry standard is 300-600 dpi, for offset print 600-1200 dpi. Electronic screens traditionally had resolutions of 72-100 dpi, but the most recent generations of tablets and smartphones feature screen resolutions of 300-600 dpi. See also Pixel.

### RTF

Acronym for Rich Text Format. A document format established in 1987 as an alternative format for Microsoft Word documents. Contrary to common belief, RTF is not an open standard and does not solve compatibility problems between word processing formats.

## S

### Server-side scripting

Server-side scripting means that, rather than transferring a previously defined web page from a web server to a web browser, the page (or part of the page) is instead dynamically generated by software running on the server. All content management systems are based on server-side scripting. A related concept is client-side scripting, where the software (for example JavaScript) is not run on the web server, but inside the user's web browser.

### Software

Structured sets of instructions to be performed by a computer or handheld device. Software can be contrasted with hardware (the actual physical device), and also with data (the information processed by the software). The terms software, computer program, application and app are often used more or less interchangeably.

### Software Development Kit (SDK)

A collection of tools and services for software developers who wish to program applications for one particular operating system or platform. SDKs are usually created by the vendors of those systems: for example, both iOS and Android have their own specific SDKs.

### Streaming

Direct audio or video playback from a website, without having to download the whole file first. Today, the most common streaming formats are MP3 and MPEG-4. Streaming requires a broadband connection to the internet, with good bandwidth. See also bandwidth.

### Style sheet

In book and journal publishing, a style sheet is an instruction document for authors that tells them which editorial conventions they need to follow while preparing their manuscript for publication. In graphic design, style sheets also refer to design templates. See Cascading Style Sheets (CSS).

### Syntax

In computing, syntax means the correct notation of a markup, command-line or programming language. Since computers cannot interpret ambiguity, 'syntax errors' easily occur in these languages; one small typo in a complex computer program will often stop the program from working altogether.

## T

### Tablet

A tablet is a compact portable computer that is operated via a touchscreen and has a larger screen than a smartphone. Apple's iPad is a typical example of a tablet computer.

### Tagging

Tags are (typically) short strings of text that contain metadata. In electronic publishing, there are two widespread forms of tags: markup tags for the (visual-typographic and logical) formatting of a document, and general metadata tags which describe and categorize the document as a whole (such as: information on the author and publisher of an ebook).

### Text editor

Software for writing and editing plain text. Unlike word processors such as Microsoft Word, text editors do not combine text writing and text formatting within one software application. Many text editors provide more powerful text processing functions than word processors, as well as specific assistance for writing in markup and programming languages.

### Unicode

Unicode is today's standard format for encoding plain text. Unlike its predecessor ASCII which is limited to the English alphabet, Unicode supports almost all writing systems. For example, classical texts of many historical written languages (such as Sanskrit) can be written in Unicode.

## W

### Word processor

Since the invention of personal computers, word processors have been among the most widely used computer software. Today's word processors like Microsoft Word and OpenOffice/LibreOffice have in fact become hybrids between text editors and desktop publishing software. However, since they work according to the WYSIWYG paradigm, the use of word processor documents in markup-oriented hybrid publishing workflows is problematic.

### WWW (World Wide Web)

Often referred to simply as the web, the WWW has become so popular that most people no longer distinguish it from the internet as a whole. The World Wide Web was created in the early 1990s as a hypertext electronic publishing system for the internet. (Before the World Wide Web, the standard internet services were e-mail, discussion groups [Usenet], chat [IRC] and file downloads [FTP].) The WWW makes use of the HTML and CSS file formats as well as the HTTP network protocol, and is accessed via web browsers.

### WYSIWYG

Acronym for What You See Is What You Get. A concept introduced with graphical user interfaces and desktop publishing in the 1980s. It means that while designing a document on a computer, it will look on the screen exactly as it will later look in print.

### XHTML

Acronym for Extensible Hypertext Markup Language. A version of HTML based on XML. It generally has the same markup as HTML, but a stricter syntax that conforms to XML rules. XHTML was supposed to supersede standard HTML for the web, but has not been widely adopted. Instead, the competing format HTML5 has become the new standard.

### XML

Acronym for Extensible Markup Language. XML is a markup language for constructing markup languages. In other words, it provides a syntax according to which specific markup languages can be built. An example of a markup language constructed with XML is XHTML. EPUB internally uses the XML-compliant 'Open Packaging Format' for cataloguing the different source files (text chapters, images etc.) used in an ebook.

## PARTICIPATING PARTNERS

B/S
B/S
B/SPUBLISHERS

CREATE-IT
APPLIED
RESEARCH

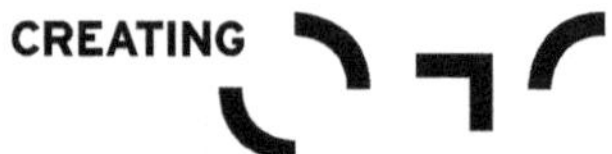

essense
RELEVANT INNOVATION

FRAM3

Hogeschool van Amsterdam

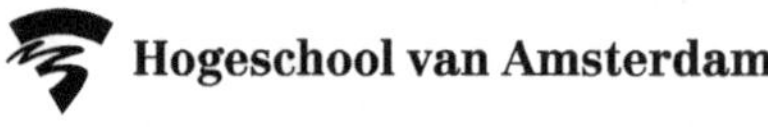

medamo

KS

MEEUSONTWERPT

Mr. Sauli

nai
010

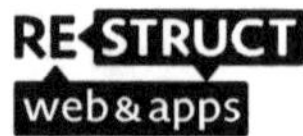

RE STRUCT
web & apps

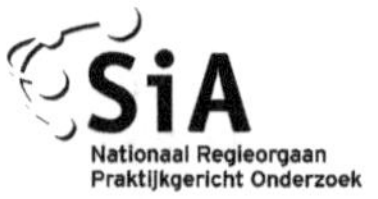

SilvioLorusso

valiz

www.ingramcontent.com/pod-product-compliance
Lightning Source LLC
La Vergne TN
LVHW010925110826
845149LV00013B/2477

* 9 7 8 9 0 8 2 2 3 4 5 3 4 *